D1162253

BARCELONA

ARCHITECTURAL DETAILS AND DELIGHTS

DISCARDED

BARCELONA
ARCHITECTURAL DETAILS AND DELIGHTS

PHOTOGRAPHS BY MELBA LEVICK

TEXT BY LLUÍS PERMANYER

EDICIONES POLÍGRAFA, S.A.

HARRY N. ABRAMS, INC., PUBLISHERS

NA
1311
.B3
L4913
1993

LIBRARY
BUNKER HILL COMMUNITY COLLEGE
CHARLESTOWN. MASS. 02129

Designed by Toni Miserachs
Translated from the Spanish by Joanna Martínez

Library of Congress Cataloging-in-Publication Data

Levick, Melba.
   [Barcelona, un paisaje modernista. English]
   Barcelona: architectural details and delights / photographs by
Melba Levick: text by Lluís Permanyer.
      p.   cm.
   Includes indexes.
   ISBN 0-8109-3125-7
   1. Art nouveau (Architecture)—Spain—Barcelona.   2. Architecture.
Modern—20th century—Spain—Barcelona.   3. Barcelona (Spain)—
Buildings, structures, etc.   I. Permanyer, L.   II. Title.
NA1311.B3L48   1993
720'. 946'72—dc20   92-30383
                                            CIP

Copyright © 1992 Ediciones Polígrafa, S.A.
Photographs copyright © 1992 Melba Levick

Published in 1993 by Ediciones Polígrafa, S.A., Barcelona,
in association with Harry N. Abrams, Incorporated, New York
A Times Mirror Company
All rights reserved. No part of the contents of this book may be
reproduced without the written permission of the publisher

Color separations: Reprocolor Llovet, S.A.
Printed by La Polígrafa, S.A., Parets del Vallès, Barcelona
Dep. Legal: B. 33.921 - 1992

CONTENTS

DEVELOPMENT OF A LANDSCAPE

When speaking of landscape, most people associate the word with the countryside. The city, however, is also a landscape, and proof of this is that for centuries painters have been attracted to and even inspired by the urban landscape. Furthermore, this urban landscape has always been associated with a varied mass of bright colours, for reality is certainly always seen as coloured, although the tones may be subdued or pale. I think this notion comes from that era when technicolour burst onto the screen and demanded that everything be bathed in colour, even though it bore little relation to the real world. For my part, I consider the essence of the urban landscape to be the streets and squares, but above all the rows of houses — in other words, the façades.

One of the distinguishing features of Barcelona, which gives it a pronounced personality on a worldwide scale, is the fact that the Eixample, the city extension laid out on the grid system by Ildefons Cerdà in the nineteenth century, contains the largest concentration in the world of buildings in the style known locally as Modernisme — the Catalan version of Art Nouveau. The area forming what is called the "Quadrat d'Or" in the Dreta de l'Eixample — or "right-hand" district of the Eixample — is a veritable Modernista landscape. And in this respect it is a gratifying experience for the urban walker or even the tourist to wander round the Eixample, for the diversity of façades is a constant source of surprise. Indeed, each house is different from the next, and each façade is adorned with countless decorative features and a wide variety of materials and motifs. I prefer, however, not to overtake events, but to present a chronological review, albeit a rapid and superficial one, in order to understand and situate this splendour within its historical framework.

The oldest existing houses in the city date from the Gothic period. In the Carrer del Correu Vell there is a thirteenth-century house, and in the Plaça de les Basses de Sant Pere a somewhat mutilated fourteenth-century one. Both give an idea of what the urban landscape was like in bygone days. At that time, the fronts of houses were barely five metres wide, a size dictated by the length of the wooden beams; and they were usually two or three stories high, nearly always covered with a flat roof. The usual building material was Montjuïc stone; the doorway was generally arched, and the windows decorated to a greater or lesser extent with columns and capitals, with a few gargoyles above.

This Gothic structure has survived to this day with a unified stone exterior, but recent research has revealed that façades were often embellished with colour, for a painted rendering was considered to provide protection against the weather.

A walk along the Carrer de Montcada is the best way of obtaining a precise idea of the appearance of an urban district in which well-to-do citizens lived, for the design and composition of the façades are all very different, despite the fact that they retain an unmistakable air of that period.

Unfortunately, Barcelona has little in the way of Renaissance architecture, since the style coincided with a decline that was to last for several hundred years. The Palau del Lloctinent in the Plaça del Rei, the Gremi de Sabaters in the Plaça de Sant Felip Neri — originally in the Carrer dels Mercaders and saved from demolition when

Casa del Gremi dels Velers. Via Laietana, 50.

Casa Cerdà. Consell de Cent / Roger de Llúria.
Example of a recently refurbished façade.

the Via Laietana was opened up — and the doorway of the church of Sant Miquel, near the church of La Mercè, are some of the few examples.

Basically, the urban environment altered very little, for the fundamental element — stone — remained the same. What changed considerably were the forms the stonecutters gave to the stone, which enable us to easily recognise the various styles.

It was during the seventeenth century that the use of ashlar blocks for the houses of prosperous families and rubble masonry for more modest dwellings began to die out. In their stead there gradually appeared an egalitarian stucco that covered the entire walls apart from the surrounds of the doors and windows, which were left in stone. Such egalitarianism on an aesthetic level also extended to a social level, for historians point out that this type of the façade applied both to mansions and to the fishermen's cottages in eighteenth century Barceloneta.

The oldest façade to have been preserved and to exhibit a decided use of colour is in the Plaça de Sant Just; it belongs to a fairly ordinary house, which makes one think it was not a pioneer of its type but that its author was copying what he had already seen.

It was the poor quality of the stucco work that lead to the eruption of sgraffito. The Ciutat Vella possesses an exceptional wealth of sgraffito, which constitutes one of its marks of identity in the same way as Modernisme does in the Eixample.

The technique of sgraffito consisted, in general, of a pattern incised on a double layer of plaster; the top layer was white and the lower layer ochre, the latter in a range of only six different tones, according to recent research by Joan Ainaud and Joan Casadevall.

It is believed that sgraffito perhaps first began to make its appearance in Barcelona at the end of the sixteenth century and certainly by the start of the following century. It is not clear whether it was the result of Italian influence, for in Italy it had already been employed since the early sixteenth century. Its moment of splendour in Catalonia was during the eighteenth century, and is explained by the desire to brighten up the gloomy façades in a period of crisis following the War of the Spanish Succession. Such splendour had the negative result of destroying earlier work, which explains why there are so few examples remaining from previous periods.

All this led to the setting up of a guild independently of the guild of painters (the *Confraria d'Estofadors, Dauradors, Esgrafiadors i Encarnadors*). Its members were simple artisans rather than real artists; they were incapable of producing new designs themselves and had to engage professional painters to stencil the decorative motifs.

The destruction of part of the Ciutat Vella with the opening up of the Via Laietana meant that the streets that disappeared and the houses that were demolished were meticulously documented, which resulted in the survey by Carreras i Candi and the collection of photographs and drawings by Dionís Baixeras, for example. I do not know whether it was the need to study the examples of sgraffito that were to disappear that also led to the exhaustive analysis of all the similarly decorated façades in the Ciutat Vella. The fact is that the volume in which the work of Carreras i Candi was published included an interesting paper by Ramon Nonat Comas.

According to Comas, the oldest sgraffito in existence is on the Casa de la Arxiconfraria de la Sang in the Plaça del Pi. It can still be seen, although it is certain to cause some astonishment, for strictly speaking it is a forerunner of sgraffito since it consists merely of rusticated, banded blocks of stone.

The most important sgraffiti in the Ciutat Vella are on the Palau Moixó in the Plaça de Sant Just; in the Plaça de la Verónica; on the Gremi dels Revenedors (1781, Louis XVI style) at Plaça del Pi number 3 — and above all, the Gremi dels Velers, executed in 1763. Its author is unknown, but it was certainly the work of an artist, for a notable feature is the use of grisaille, adding shading and relief to the large female figures presiding over the façade.

An example of the use of classical reliefs on an eclectic façade.

The use of sgraffito was so widespread that it can almost be considered a distinguishing feature of the architecture of Barcelona and Catalonia.

The Neo-classical reaction was not long in coming and, as usual, it was a complete contrast, to the extent that sgraffito practically disappeared. This new style — new in the sense of change, for in truth it was a backward-looking ransacking of history — showed a certain megalomania, combined with pretence. In fact, as the use of ashlar blocks declined, the employment of building materials of the most prosaic sort was camouflaged with stucco that imitated stonework or marble. It was at this time that the use of terracotta ornamentation became prevalent. The appearance of these reliefs in baked clay can be explained by the desire to possess sculptural works, despite the fact that most people lacked the means to pay for what in earlier centuries was produced by carving in stone. To a certain extent it was the result of wishful thinking. Such falseness was carried to the extreme by painting terracotta in such a way as to resemble marble.

The baked clay was decorated in workshops that soon made a name for themselves, such as Tarrés, Massana, Antonés, Fita and Santigosa in Barcelona, and those of Pere Muixí and Josep Escaiola in Sabadell.

Representative Neo-classical buildings are the Llotja, the new façade of the City Hall, and the Labyrinth in Horta. As regards house fronts, these had the appearance of stone, followed traditional window patterns, and the walls were the favourite areas for the minimal ornamentation in terracotta, often vertical in form and inspired by the banal themes of the Rococo. Decorative cast-iron pieces were also added.

Only the new theories propounded by the Modernista artists would put an end to all this.

The first stuccoed façade was that of the Customs House, which dates from 1792. This technique became so prevalent that it was almost the only one in existence between 1835 and 1850, provoking the following caustic comment from Manuel Angelón in his satirical guide to the city: "Ever since owners became obsessed with stucco, painters have discovered so many new marbles and jaspers . . . that, between sky blue and orange, there are only ill-chosen colours and even worse combinations. For imitating marble, it has been decided that all colours are acceptable except white."

The first façades painted *al fresco* were those of the Nou Palau del Bisbe in the Plaça Nova (1782). This was the work of the renowned artist of the period, Francesc Pla, popularly known as "El Vigatà", who followed the latest French Baroque tradition. The paintings, which were placed between the windows, were highly praised as soon as they were seen by the astonished citizens of Barcelona; no trace of them remains.

Three years later, the Palau Moja was similarly decorated in order to outshine the recent Palau de la Virreina. The work was begun by "El Vigatà", who painted the back of the building, and was completed by Flaugier on the front giving on to the Rambla.

Sectarian politics also came into play in the design of façades. The liberal fervour of 1823 emptied the niches of their saints and virgins and replaced them with plaques inscribed with the articles of the Constitution, in the hopes that the people would learn them by heart. The plaques appeared on the façades of both houses and churches. This obsession led to a proposal to complete the façade of the cathedral — which was only erected in 1888, thanks to the munificence of Manuel Girona — on the basis of such Constitutional plaques in white marble. Had this idea actually been implemented, it would have been a premonition of Surrealism. The royalist occupation by the Hundred Thousand Children of St. Louis put an end to such nonsense, although some of these plaques remained in existence until only a short time ago and a few can still be found, somewhat defaced, such as the one on the church of Betlem.

Romanticism brought virtually no changes to the external appearance of façades. The timid use of colour can occasionally be seen, and there are a couple of examples

The oldest example of sgraffito.
Plaça del Pi, 1.

Civil Governor's office. Pla de Palau.

in the Plaça Reial and on the Casa Xifré where restoration work has highlighted the colouring.

It was prior to Modernisme and parallel with the fading Eclecticism that designs were assiduously inspired by exotic subjects, perhaps provoked by the urge to discover new worlds.

The Casa Quadros, by the architect Josep Vilaseca, is the fruit of a journey he made to the Far East. In Japan he had the opportunity of attending a large exhibition, where he bought an album or catalogue from which he practically copied the Japanese themes that enabled him to produce such curious panels. The overall effect is astonishing, particularly with the dragon on the corner leaping into space with unusual bravado. When the great poet Josep Carner occasionally returned from exile during the Franco regime he was sadly already suffering from senile dementia and did not realise that he was actually in the city of his birth, but I am not surprised by the fact that on re-encountering this fabled animal he made some remark that confirmed his awareness that he was indeed in Barcelona. This is a story that shows to what extent we are influenced by the urban landscape.

It is therefore understandable to find in the middle of the Eixample nothing less than a house inspired by Chinese architecture, in Carrer del Consell de Cent near the corner of Muntaner. And there is also a Roman temple, the Taller Masriera at Carrer de Bailèn 72, for the silversmiths there considered their work to merit the category of a sacred ritual.

But the most widespread of the exotic styles was the Neo-Arabic, though for obvious reasons neither in Barcelona nor in Catalonia did it ever achieve the importance that it attained in the rest of Spain. Although few examples remain, for the action of the pickaxes has been implacable, at Passeig de Gràcia 24 is the Casa Pere Llibre designed by the master builders Domènec Balet and Pere Bassegoda i Mateu, though with the ground floor appallingly mutilated. The Neo-Arabism that was practised here placed special emphasis on decorative details based on geometry rather than on polychromy. This is a pity, and it is interesting to remember that the great architect Josep Puig i Cadafalch declared himself to be against such examples of an architecture that had nothing to do with historical Catalan roots, an opinion he expressed in the early days of Modernisme, when the debate on what path that renovating style should follow in Catalonia was intensifying.

While Art Nouveau — to use what is perhaps the most common of the many terms employed, for each country produced its own and hence we have Sezessionstil, Jugendstil, Art Nouille, Stile Liberty, Modern Style, Art 1900 — was an avant-garde art strictly driven by purely aesthetic aims, Catalan Modernisme contributed an essentially human base, which explains how it put down so many and such strong roots here, enjoyed a popularity never experienced abroad and achieved an astounding degree of splendour. A whole variety of historical, economic and sociological circumstances occurred together with a rare unanimity, and clearly account for the result.

The existence of a large site, the product of an area on which the War Ministry had until then prohibited any building, permitted the layout and construction of the Eixample. The local bourgeoisie entered a period of economic boom. After several centuries of decline, Catalonia — and Barcelona in particular — experienced a political revival and needed to re-establish the signs of its mediaeval splendour. The explosive situation in the colonies forced not a few wealthy individuals who had made their fortunes in Cuba to return to their homeland, where part of their capital was invested in the building of large houses. Leading rural families, tired of an interminable civil war that was rapidly ruining them financially, sold their properties and also settled in the Eixample. Catalan nationalism arose from its ashes and went in search of its marks of identity. Due to one of those favourable, unrepeatable accidents of history, all this coincided

Rambla, 166 / Portaferrissa.

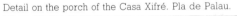

Detail on the porch of the Casa Xifré. Pla de Palau.

with the birth of a great artistic style that manifested itself in all the creative fields, but in Barcelona was to be employed mainly in architecture and the applied arts. It would have been unfortunate indeed if all these events had occurred under Eclecticism or some equally mediocre style, instead of Modernisme.

The pioneer Modernista buildings that presaged that great explosion were, among others, Editorial Montaner y Simón by Domènech i Montaner; the Acadèmia de Ciències, by Domènech i Estapà; Indústries d'Art F. Vidal, by Vilaseca; and Casa Pla, by Valeri i Pupurull.

In a city that seemed to be recovering from its decline, the challenge of organising the 1888 Universal Exhibition gave an added boost to the initial impulse. Two buildings for the exhibition that were to have a notable influence were the Arc de Triomf by Vilaseca, and the Cafè-Restaurant by Domènech i Montaner. Both were built of brick, a modular material that characterised an era, but historically a very Catalan building material, for the shallow brick vault was the local interpretation of the *volta a foglio* in Volterra. The immediate forerunners as far as works of architecture are concerned had been the Casa Vicens by Gaudí and Editorial Montaner y Simón. The immediate result, as perceived by the passer-by, was an eye-catching splash of bright colour, for in addition to standing out against the surrounding grey, the red brick could well withstand the polluted urban atmosphere and the passing of time. That strong stroke of colour in the middle of the city announced the imminent outbreak of a hitherto unknown polychromy that was to pave the way for Modernisme. The use of brick showed a desire for naturalness, a reaction against the cosmetic renderings and mediocre imitations that had characterised earlier periods. Brick took hold in Barcelona sometime after Morris's Red House (1859) but before Berlage's Amsterdam Stock Exchange, and this fact has still not been recognised by critics on an international level. Brick was also what today would be considered a "poor" material, but for the first time it was shown in all its nakedness. In the same order of things, the use of baked clay in sculptures — Editorial Montaner y Simón — and in reliefs — Acadèmia de Ciències — was no longer camouflaged under paintwork that tried to pass it off as a fine material.

Modernisme here was of a longer duration and more profoundly established than in other countries, though art historians define the period with notable discrepancies: Ràfols considers it to have been born in 1888 and to have died away in 1907; Bohigas, to have run from 1888-1924; Bassegoda, 1875-1930; Collins, 1870-1930.

It is worth describing an ordinary eclectic house in order to see the change introduced by Modernisme. It was usually of a functional design with little ornamentation, since it was constructed by a builder and then put up for sale. Thus, the absence of an owner who might have wished to imprint his personality on it explains the proliferation of so many similar house fronts in the Eixample, designed at first merely on the basis of rows of windows but later invariably composed of a balanced pattern of simple balconies. The façade, generally plain and in the middle of a terrace of non-uniform buildings, had on average a width of around fourteen metres, between three and five balconies, and the front door set in the centre. Houses generally had semi-basements, a mezzanine floor or *entresol*, the *piano nobile* or *principal* floor, and two or three further stories. The façade was usually of brick clad in stone — so as to appear to be something other than what it actually was. The balconies had an overhang of only 80 centimetres. The roof was flat, with a balustrade across the front. The exterior woodwork was of *melis* (a type of pine), and the shutters were always of the casement type.

Modernisme introduced innovations in the composition and ornamentation of façades and particularly in the crests or parapets. I see no point in describing them, for thanks to the skill of photographer Melba Levick the following pages provide the fullest testimony in colour ever published in a book.

Casa del Gremi dels Revenedors.
Plaça del Pi, 3.

There are those who believe that the applied arts developed as a result of Modernisme. In fact it was precisely the reverse, for as a consequence of the strong local tradition in all the applied arts, the architects immediately found craftsmen able to materialise their designs. Like the architects, when it came to decorating the façades, these craftsman had to limit the use of colours to those available on the market.

Catalonia, and in particular Barcelona, had guilds of a high standing that were firmly established in the social fabric. For economic reasons, and also for reasons of human nature, the craftsmen were still tied to their workbenches, and the surge of Modernisme caught them, quite literally, working. Despite this, immediately after the Universal Exhibition in 1888, the Cafè-Restaurant de la Exposició was converted by Domènech i Montaner into a centre for applied arts, in which attempts were made to modernise working methods that had been handed down for centuries. A tight-knit group was formed, in the belief that its members could contribute decisively to the reconstruction of the country. It was recalled in the following terms by Domènech i Montaner in 1903, in an article on the architect Gallissà published in Catalan in *La Veu de Catalunya*, the daily newspaper of the Lliga Regionalista: "At that time, I was engaged on the Comillas project, and the then mayor Coll i Pujol wanted to finish what was known as the Cafè-Restaurant or Castell dels Tres Dragons in the park; to get rid of that air of abandonment, of work left unfinished through lack of funds or lack of interest, that all our municipal buildings have; and it was there that I set up our workshop. We tried to revive applied arts and techniques — bronze casting and wrought ironwork, terracotta and ceramics gilded in the Valencian manner, repoussé work on metal, maiolica tiles, wood carving and decorative sculpture, which were then being done in a very poor, rudimentary way. Gallissà never stopped for a single moment, running back and forth between our studio and the workshops. We had assembled a group of people, then mainly beginners and now leading names in Catalan arts and crafts, whom we tried to train in architectural work."

Among others were the sculptors Eusebi Arnau and Quintana. Gaudí and Domènech travelled to Manises near Valencia, where the old ceramicist Gassany revealed to them the secrets of his kilns so that they could adapt them to their own needs. The mosaic artists Mario Maragliano and Lluís Bru managed to produce Roman, Arab and Venetian — Bru had done a course in Venice — specialities as well as *trencadís*, the Catalan mosaic formed of fragments of glazed pottery.

That central nucleus and the involvement of its members in the early architectural works acted with the speed and efficiency of an oil slick.

In the field of wrought iron they achieved wonders, but it should not be forgotten that back in the Middle Ages Catalan craftsmen had acquired such international renown that their crossbows had been admired in Europe since 1292; in 1381 the king of Portugal purchased arrows from them, the Duke of Alba ordered all his arms from Catalonia in 1547, and it is said that even the grilles of Notre Dame were made here. Manuel Ballarín, the former blacksmith, became the forger whom Falqués preferred to work with, and he designed the lampposts for the Passeig de Gràcia, Cinc d'Oros and Saló de Sant Joan; Esteve Andorrà worked closely with Puig i Cadafalch. Other distinguished craftsmen were Ibáñez, Torrebadell, Basons, Moià, Casademunt and Mariano Rifà. Masriera i Campins emerged as the leader in artistic casting, though the firms of Costa y Ponces, Miret y Ascent, Bertrán y Torras and G. Florensa were also renowned for metalwork.

With regard to tiles we should mention Hermanos Oliva; Torres, Mauri y Cía.; and in particular Pujol i Bausis. Mateo Cullell was also a mosaic and tile designer.

Hermenegildo Miralles was able to make perfect papier-maché imitations, such as those that decorated the sumptuous Café Torino on the corner of Passeig de Gràcia and Gran Via.

A typical example of terracotta relief.

Ornamental detail on the Casa Xifré.

Amigó, Rigalt, Bordalba and Vilella produced a wonderful world of stained-glass windows, worthy successors to the Gothic.

"Industrial art is an art that must be taken as seriously as the art of painting a picture or sculpting a figure; it should not be forgotten that in such developed countries as England, geniuses like William Morris think nothing of designing a tile," wrote the enlightened Alexandre de Riquer in 1903 in the review *Joventut*. It must be acknowledged that no architects considered they were demeaning themselves by applying their creative talents to the most varied aspects of the applied arts. On the contrary, it demonstrated that they were complete artists, in the sense that they could as easily design a large house as sketch the ornamental details of a façade. This was part of the greatness of Modernisme, for the utmost attention was devoted to all the minor and most prosaic aspects of its most trivial details.

Another of the innovative features of Modernisme, to my mind, was the importance it attached to colour. I think that one would have to go back in the history of architecture as far as the Greeks to find such a rich and vivid polychromy. I know it is not true that architects had previously designed only in black and white, although appearances would seem to confirm the opposite. I say this because perusal of the muncipal archives might give such an impression to the uninformed person, for in order to simplify their work they used to present plans drawn only in ink. However, it is a well known fact that plans for clients were produced in colour, although I have the idea that this was to facilitate understanding and to give a better impression of the building to be constructed. The fact is that when looking at certain buildings, particularly those in which only stone has been used, I find it hard to believe that the architect would employ a specific type of material on account of its contribution to the overall colour scheme rather than because of its intrinsic quality; the sensibilities of such architects have nothing to do with the sensibilities of a craftsman skilled in marquetry. In this respect, certain architects seem to be basically cabinet-makers; this is not a criticism, for Borromini was one of them — it is a question of character, style and personality.

The Modernista architects went in for colour; they understood it in all its dimensions and they used it with an audaciousness that has not been seen since, for recent Post-Modernist gems seem palid and timid beside them. A whole façade in red, as Sagnier demonstrated, shows confidence in the result and also in oneself. A richer colouring than that achieved by Granell in the building at Carrer de Girona 122, by Gaudí in the Casa Batlló or by Valeri i Pupurull on the back of the Casa Comalat is unimaginable. But the Modernista architects also brought colour — soft tones, but colour nonetheless — to wrought iron, whether in the lampposts designed by Falqués, Gaudí's balconies for the Casa Batlló or those by Jujol for La Pedrera. The woodwork was yet one more feature on the overall façade — nearly always green, although later a darkish ochre was to become popular. They also incorporated ceramic and sgraffito, and managed to exploit both genres to the full.

It is not therefore an exaggeration to say that the Modernista designers worked with a large palette of colours; hence the spectacular richness of the urban landscape of Barcelona.

Years ago, this city gave the impression of being more grey than dirty, but the effectiveness of the imaginative and seductive municipal campaign *"Barcelona, posa't guapa"* (Barcelona, doll yourself up) very soon showed the amazed citizens that it was really more dirty than grey. The first façades to be restored overwhelmingly confirmed this, to the point that the magnificent photographs by Melba Levick could not have been taken unless this campaign had been successful.

It was the painter Léger, with his innate sensibility, who said that "The reds save London". The touches of colour provided by the buses, the telephone boxes, the guardsmen's tunics, are a vibrating counterpoint in an environment that tends towards

The Teatre Principal in the Rambla, Barcelona's oldest theatre.

gloomy colours — with the exception of the pure white district of Belgravia. This remark was an acknowledgement of the effectiveness of colour in the urban landscape; and thanks to Modernisme, the landscape of Barcelona is of unparalleled originality.

The Noucentisme that immediately followed Modernisme was an impoverishment in every sense, both in the standard of architecture and in the decoration of the façades. The aesthetic advocated by Eugeni d'Ors called for moderation, reason, order — all Mediterranean qualities. The bourgeoisie has always used the Mediterranean as an excuse to justify its conservative tendencies. One of the most interesting aspects of this period, which continued until the Spanish Civil War, was the stucco, which was naturally less spectacular and less colourful than that of the preceding style. The curved façade of the Coliseum cinema (1923) by Francesc de P. Nebot is especially unusual, the only previous example being the Teatre Principal in the Rambles.

The worst aspect of Noucentisme was the way in which it discredited Modernisme. It upset the Noucentista architects so much that they proposed purely and simply demolishing the Modernista buildings, and the more of them the better. This is the explanation for the mutilation and destruction suffered by so many of them before the laissez-faire attitude of the municipal authorities, particularly the city councils during the Franco regime. They tolerated the demolition squads, they allowed façades of considerable artistic value to be disfigured by lopping off the parapet and adding a few more stories, without the least attempt to harmonise such grotesque additions; they permitted ground floor ornamentation to be stripped off and modern shop-fronts installed, thus spoiling the consistency and balance of the façades of the buildings.

The disappearance of Puig i Cadafalch's Casa Trinxet and the mutilation of Domènech i Montaner's Casa Lleó i Morera are two prime examples of the irreparable damage caused in the Eixample by the militants of Noucentisme. Domènech i Montaner's Casa Fuster and Rubió i Bellver's Casa de Golferichs were saved thanks to popular lobbying.

The regulations governing the *"Barcelona, posa't guapa"* campaign, prohibiting any decoration not in keeping with the façade, particularly three-dimensional items, have been a step in the right direction, contributing to the recovery of the most visible and vital parts of the house fronts.

During the years of the Republic, a group of avant-garde architects introduced Rationalism. One of the façades I find most attractive is the one designed by Folguera for Tecla Sala, known as the Casal Sant Jordi. The whole front is a metallic greenish-grey, with marbled window and door surrounds providing the necessary contrast. A bold work of considerable interest.

In the immediate postwar years, the main shopping area and nerve centre of the Eixample — Plaça de Catalunya and Passeig de Gràcia — was invaded by the nondescript, pompous, dictatorial architecture of the banks. There is no forgiving them, for with all the money in the world to spend on designing their headquarters, they employed not the best architects but rather mediocre and, what is more, pretentious ones. The result meant the demolition of interesting buildings, the impoverishment of the urban landscape and the removal of the shops, which all contributed to killing off city life. This is the reason why Rambla de Catalunya became the principal shopping street.

The chaotic proliferation of television aerials has spoilt the skyline and the crests of the façades. I hope that cable television will help to erradicate this horrible spectacle.

The recent municipal regulations relating to the historical centre of the Eixample — which require, for example, certain façades to be preserved but allow the rest of the building to be destroyed — could, to my mind, be disastrous. Not only are they a licence for falseness and pretence, but they prevent present-day architects from giving the best of themselves, for they are obliged to incorporate remains of little or no value. This is the case of the eclectic Palau Vedruna and also the Casa Pau Salvat. It would be more honest and straightforward to decide once and for all whether or not these buildings are to be preserved, for the Eixample has always been characterised by freedom of expression at all times. Indeed, Gaudí, Puig and Domènech all demolished buildings of little interest in order to erect their avant-garde creations. The city is a living, changing thing, and each style must be allowed to make its mark. The Banca Catalana building in Passeig de Gràcia, designed by Tous i Fargas, was one such marker, and its modern style fits in well with the surroundings. I am all in favour of letting the current avant-garde erect its designs in the Eixample; it is more important to deal decisively and effectively with the ugliness of the bare party-walls.

The colour chart established in 1991 is an acknowledgement of the rich architectural heritage of Barcelona that became evident when the massive restoration of façades was undertaken. It will mean the definitive consolidation of that Barcelona landscape that has found its greatest and most spectacular expression in the Eixample — a landscape that reminds me of the sea in that however long one looks and looks one never tires of it, for it is a constant source of new sensations.

CASA ROMÀ MACAYA I GIBERT

1902
Josep Puig i Cadafalch (1867-1957),
Architect
Passeig de Sant Joan, 108

Designed in 1901. Collaborators: Eusebi Arnau, sculptor; Alfons Juyol, decorative stonework; Joan Paradís, sgraffito; Pujol i Bausis, ceramics; Manuel Ballarín and Esteve Andorrà, wrought-ironwork. Considered one of the best houses built in 1902.

Puig i Cadafalch designed it in a style that he had often employed before with excellent results: it had the appearance of a family mansion, although it was in fact an apartment building.

Of the houses designed at that time by this leading Modernista architect, it is one of the most austere yet elegant, with a predominance of pristine white. In addition, in the ornamentation he used glazed ceramic and sgraffito, for which he frequently admitted a predilection.

It is curious to observe the capital dedicated to the bicycle — an evocative, endearing detail, for at the time the architect was also working on the construction of the Casa Amatller and used to travel between Passeig de Gràcia and Passeig de Sant Joan on one such delightful two-wheeler.

It is worth repeating the judgement pronounced by the architect and critic Pujol i Brull, who declared how impressed he was that Puig i Cadafalch had the talent to give to "a building for domestic use, and therefore one with rather unsuitable external forms, a lively and entirely different character; with the indispensable balustrade on the roof, the meticulous rows of balconies, and the other circumstances equally unfavourable to the architect's freedom of action. In such a struggle, he has been victorious", thanks to the fact that the artist is "above all sincere" and, as such, "with this gift, his buildings will be his image".

This building is classified by Alexandre Cirici as belonging to the architect's pink period, in view of the fact that it came between two houses built of brick: Casa Martí and Casa Terrades. He considers it to be characterised by a rural patriarchalism, a veneration of the *casa pairal* or country house, associating these forms with those of the *masia*. The Casa Macaya thus takes on the air of a typical rural house, with its arched windows, but with the wall tiles, roof tiles and sgraffito to monumentalise it.

The running balcony, the window crests and the elaborately worked oriel window are the most noteworthy features of the ornamental stonework, while the sgraffito shows the architect's latent tendency towards the Baroque that was soon to flourish in the design of the Palau Quadras.

Badly damaged inside after being used as a school for the disabled, the building was acquired by the Caixa d'Estalvis i Pensions de Barcelona in the late 1970's and was duly restored.

CASA JOSEP J. BERTRAND

1904
Enric Sagnier i Villavecchia (1858-1931),
Architect
Balmes, 44-48

Designed in 1902. The Modernistes mastered colour as nobody else. This simple red gives a strong personality to the façade; but if we look hard, there is much excellent stonework all over it. Of all the reliefs, I prefer the subtle one of floral inspiration gracing the spaces between the balconies. This house was part of a property investment operation by the owner — hence its similarity to the buildings at Balmes 50 and Consell de Cent 274, also designed in the same year.

CASA DOLORS XIRÓ, VÍDUA DE VALLET

1912
Josep Barenys i Gambús (1875-1953),
Architect
Mallorca, 302

Designed in 1913. A harmonious treatment in which attention must be drawn to the formal relationship between the oval windows on the *entresol* and the purely ornamental round aperture on the crest. Good decorative work in wrought-iron and stone on the balconies, both on the principal floor and above the two oriel windows.

CASA MARTÍ LLORENS

1906
Antoni Alabern i Pomar,
Master Builder
València, 213

Designed in 1904. A balanced, restrained façade of stone with a varied and original texture. Despite being the work of a master builder, who generally tends to be mainly associated with the structural elements, certain highly conspicuous ornamental details can be noted. The wrought-ironwork on the balconies is of high quality, despite its austerity, and the undersides of the balconies are a good example of decorative stonework. The crest, underlined by four medallions and the twin wrought-iron pulleys for hoisting up furniture, is perhaps the most ornamental feature, designed on the basis of curves. All in all, the decoration on this house has a very individual personality, for it is the only one with polychrome floral reliefs framing the windows — on the top floor, strangely enough, since it is normally the lower floors that are the most highly decorated, with the exception of the crest. The ornamental work on the oriel windows had deteriorated so badly that it has unfortunately disappeared. Special care was taken with the woodwork and stained-glass windows; and the front door is one of the most beautiful to be seen. It should be noted, however, that the woodwork and stained-glass have recently been replaced by reproductions of a commendable fidelity.

CASA JOSEP BATLLÓ I CASANOVAS

1906
Antoni Gaudí i Cornet (1852-1926),
Architect
Passeig de Gràcia, 43

Designed in 1904. Selected by the jury for the City Council prizes as one of the best houses constructed in 1906. Those collaborating on the façade included Josep Maria Jujol and Joan Rubió i Bellver, architects; Tallers Pelegrí, stained-glass windows; Germans Badia, metalwork; Casas i Bardés, carpentry; Fills de J. Pujol i Bausis and Sebastià Ribó, ceramics. Gaudí was commissioned to remodel the house built by the architect Emili Sala i Cortés in 1875. The most substantial changes were to the façade, entrance, staircase, principal floor, light well and ground-floor shops.

This façade is the most original, the most creative and the most expressive in the entire city. Two interpretations have been profferred as to the theme that Gaudí possibly tried to evoke.

According to the first, the crest represents a harlequin's cap, the abstract polychromy of the rest of the façade suggests falling confetti, and the balconies would be the masks — a theme closely associated with Carnival. I find it hard to believe that Gaudí the misogynist and fervent believer would have been attracted by such a frivolity, which at that time was also openly anti-religious.

The second reading, on the other hand, considers the upper part to be the dragon's spine; the tower, crowned with the typical three-dimensional cross, is the lance of St. George — patron saint of Catalonia — thrust into the body of the incarnation of evil, as demonstrated by the aperture-wound in red, clearly visible on the right-hand side. The rest of the façade represents the dragon's scales; while the balconies are pieces of skulls — the apertures denote the eye sockets, and the central hole at the base marks the nose — and the bone-like forms on the ground and first two floors are the femurs, patellas, tibias and fibulas of the victims devoured by the mythical creature. This interpretation not only seems to me to be closer to reality and to Gaudí's artistic concepts, but the people of Barcelona also immediately interpreted it in this way, for on the day after the official opening they began to call it the "house of bones". Hence the fact that the original colour of the balconies was ivory, the colour of bones, rather than the black in which they were painted after the Civil War until the excellent restoration in 1984 returned them to their initial colour.

Although it cannot be proved, I am inclined to think that the flat, abstract façade, rather than the crest, was designed by the brilliant architect Josep Maria Jujol, and that he used some of the ceramic discs to decorate the curving benches in the Park Güell. I think this building is closer to the characteristic style of Jujol than to that of Gaudí.

CASA FERRAN CORTÉS

1902
Enric Sagnier i Villavecchia (1858-1931),
Architect
Rambla de Catalunya, 96

Designed in 1900. The central, symmetrical oriel window dominates this façade constructed of stone. Notable features are the two female heads, sculpted along lines obviously influenced by Art Nouveau, which fulfil a clearly decorative mission rather than acting as effective support for the oriel. The overall aesthetic effect of the façade was greatly spoilt by the two stories that were so obviously added on.

CASA BOBÉS

1904
Balmes, 30

The characteristic green colour of Modernisme is employed here in the same bold way as it was used by Sagnier on the houses at Balmes 44-48, Balmes 50 and Consell de Cent 274. The architect who designed this house also successfully harmonised the green with the pink of the sgraffito.

CASES CASTILLO VILLANUEVA

1909
Juli Fossas i Martínez (1868-1945),
Architect
Roger de Llúria, 80 / Valencia, 312

Designed in 1904. It is a pity that the present asymmetry is the result of the mutilation of both the tower and the ornamentation on the delightful balconies on the València corner, for the design of these balconies is precisely the most original of all those in the Quadrat d'Or. The oriel windows were embellished with stained-glass and decorative metalwork.

EDITORIAL MONTANER Y SIMÓN

1886
Lluís Domènech i Montaner (1849-1923),
Architect
Aragó, 255

Designed in 1879. This was the first large building by the leading architect of Modernisme, for I consider Gaudí to be an expressionist. But it was also one of the first outstanding buildings in a style as yet in its infancy though shortly to predominate. According to the renowned architect and treatise writer Oriol Bohigas, the Editorial Montaner y Simón is one of the five buildings that marked the break with Classicism, Eclecticism and Mediaevalism; the other four are the Casa Vicens by Gaudí, the Museu Biblioteca Balaguer (in Vilanova i la Geltrú) by Granell, the Acadèmia de Ciències by Domènech i Estapà, and Indústries d'Art Francesc Vidal by Vilaseca.

Domènech i Montaner was commissioned to design this building by his cousin Ramon de Montaner and his partner Francesc Simon as the headquarters of their printing and publishing business. It was a considerable challenge, for erecting an industrial building in such a central part of the middle-class district of the Dreta de l'Eixample was not at all easy. However, Domènech i Montaner rose to the occasion.

He first designed a stone façade, then reconsidered it and finally decided to do something new and very different, for in addition to designing it entirely in brick he had the courage not to plaster over a single part of it. This was one of the characteristic features that distinguished the Modernista architects: the avoidance of any pretence or dissimulation. Moreover, brick was better suited to letting the outside appearance indicate what the structure actually was: an industrial building. But his treatment of this material showed his extraordinary gifts as an architect, for he designed the building with an ornamentation almost more appropriate to a private house. In fact, he used nothing but brick to achieve the decorative effects, forming patterns in relief that recalled the Islamic world.

The crest of the façade is the most elaborate part. He used unpainted terracotta as a sign of respect for the qualities of the material, and he audaciously employed cement for something as delicate as the central motif. It was a bold act that paid off.

On the crest is the publisher's mark in the centre of the three rosettes in the form of cogwheels; among the heraldic elements are the compass and book, symbols of the trade, together with the five-point star and the eagle, of progressive leanings; at the apex is a helmet. The busts are of Dante, Cervantes and Shakespeare. Alongside them are the names of Malte-Brun, progressive French geographer; Lafuente, historian; Secchi, Italian astronomer; and a fourth that has never been decyphered, even when the building was being restored.

The name of the publishing house was sculpted round the architrave of the main doorway, a solution that was copied by the architects of the Palau de Justícia and the Hospital Clínic.

Although the wrought-ironwork is interesting, it is the grilles on the ground floor that merit special attention, for they were the pioneers of the Modernista whiplash curves that were soon to inundate Barcelona. Stained-glass was used in the windows.

Since 1990 the building has been the seat of the Tàpies Foundation, the conversion being the work of the architects Roser Amadó and Lluís Domènech. Antoni Tàpies himself created a daringly beautiful sculpture in wire that serves to overcome the ugly problem of the great difference in height between the Foundation and the buildings on either side of it.

50

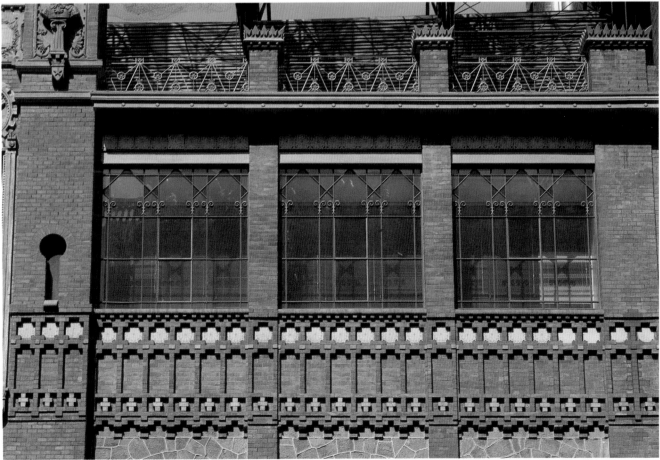

EDITORIAL MONTANER Y SIMÓN

CASA JOSEP FILELLA

1911
Manuel J. Raspall i Mayol (1877-1937),
Architect
Balmes, 149 / Còrsega, 283

Designed in 1909. The building originally had oriel windows on the corners. During recent restoration work it was discovered that it had been built by this outstanding architect. Despite the fact that his work was always distinguished by the use of applied arts, the design for this house was based solely and exclusively on stone. It is the only apartment building he designed in Barcelona, his other works being a shop and a theatre — Teixidor in the Ronda de Sant Pere and El Molino.

PALAU RAMON DE MONTANER

1893
Josep Domènech i Estapà (1858-1917),
Architect
Mallorca, 278

Designed in 1889. Collaborators: Eusebi Arnau, sculptor; Becchini, sculptural ornamentation; Antoni Rigalt, stained-glass windows; Planas i Tort, carpentry.

Immediately after their business headquarters had been constructed, the owners of the Editorial Montaner y Simón decided to have a mansion built for each of them. They were both erected on the same street, one on the corner of Roger de Llúria, and the other, belonging to Francesc Simon — now demolished — in an identical position on the corner of Pau Clarís. They were large detached houses surrounded by spacious gardens. This one has fortunately been saved and is something of a rarity: it is the only completely detached mansion with a garden in a corner position — preventing any adjacent construction with party walls — that exists in the whole of the Eixample.

It was designed by Josep Domènech i Estapà, but after construction had commenced a serious dispute arose between owner and architect, and the latter was replaced by his relative Lluís Domènech i Montaner, the architect of the publishing house, who then took charge of the construction work and was also responsible for designing the top floor and the decoration. This fact is important, for it is precisely this floor that contains the greater part of the ornamental work, whereas the Palau Simon (1886) was distinguished by its austerity. In the decoration, Domènech i Montaner was assisted by the architect Gallissà, who was his right-hand man in that centre for applied arts that was set up at the end of the Universal Exhibition of 1888 and is today the Zoological Museum in the Parc de la Ciutadella.

Doors and windows were embellished with stained glass. Large subtle panels of metallic glazed mosaic, in the manner of a huge frieze running just below the eaves, depict the story of Gutenberg's invention of printing in the Western world. They are works of a quality on a par with oil painting, such is the perfection achieved in this particular branch of the applied arts.

The main door is adorned with an eagle

carved in stone, flanked by two shields showing the year in which the house was completed.

The wall round the property is decorated with linear incisions in the stone. The wrought-iron railings surmounting the wall are finely worked, and even finer are the large iron doors. The lamps are also highly decorative. These external surrounds of the house had already been drawn by Domènech i Estapà.

The architect Marc Carbonell was responsible for the restoration of the outside and remodelling of the interior in 1980 to convert the building into the seat of the Delegado del Gobierno (the central government's delegate) in Catalonia.

CASA MANUEL FELIP

1903
Telm Fernández i Janot (?-1926),
Ausiàs Marc, 20

Designed in 1901. Sumptuous work in stone. One's eye is drawn to the robust carving on the balconies, particularly on the principal floor. A rich ornamentation typical of the Quadrat d'Or, in which one of the more notable streets was the Carrer de Ausiàs Marc.

CASA FRANCESC DE P. VALLET

1919
Gabriel Borrrell i Cardona,
Architect
Bailèn, 36

Designed in 1908. Despite the late date of the building, it has a markedly Modernista façade, for although a number of problems delayed construction for some years, the original plans were carefully adhered to. The oriel window is perhaps the immediate focus of attention, but it is by no means the most outstanding feature of the façade. There is some fine ornamental stonework, mainly framing the front door and the balconies with their delicate wrought-iron railings. The parapet, in my view, is of particular interest with its unusual and imaginative wrought-ironwork.

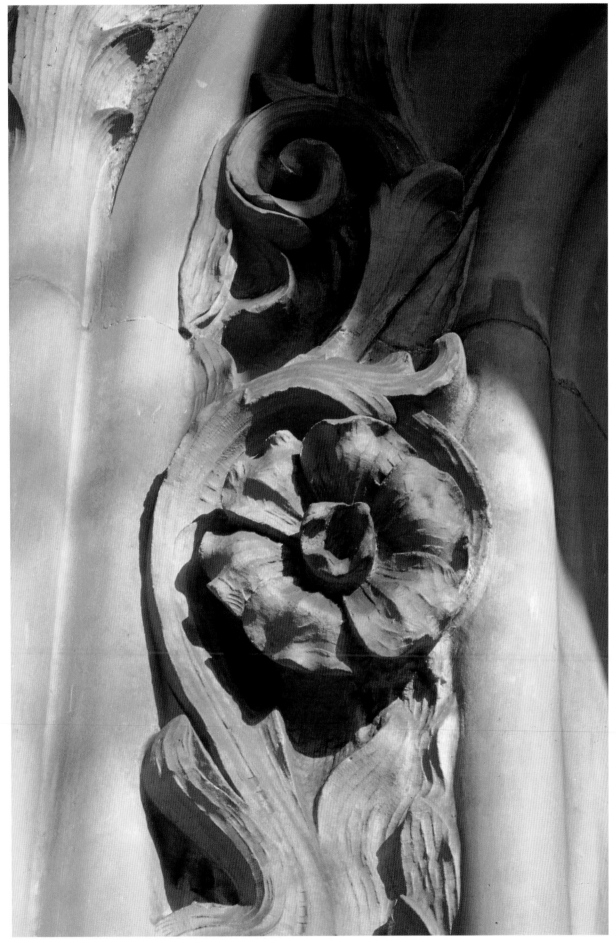

CASA ISABEL POMAR

1906
Joan Rubió i Bellver (1871-1952),
Architect
Girona, 86

The plans were drawn up in 1904. Rubió showed his calibre as an architect in designing this delightful house on such a narrow plot, which limited the development of the façade. The most striking feature is the staggered oriel window with its sculptural underside. A fruitful dialogue is established between the unusual green ceramic and the wrought-ironwork, with the bright red brick adding a lively touch. Also noteworthy is the Neo-Gothic pinnacle.

CASA JACINTA RUIZ

1909
Ramon Viñolas i Llosas (1868-?),
Architect
Girona, 54

Designed in 1904. While an oriel window is generally an essential feature of any Modernista façade, in this building the four-storey oriel is the pivot on which the architect has based his design. In addition to the three-dimensional force of the façade, the floral decoration in stone and wrought-iron on the balconies is particularly outstanding.

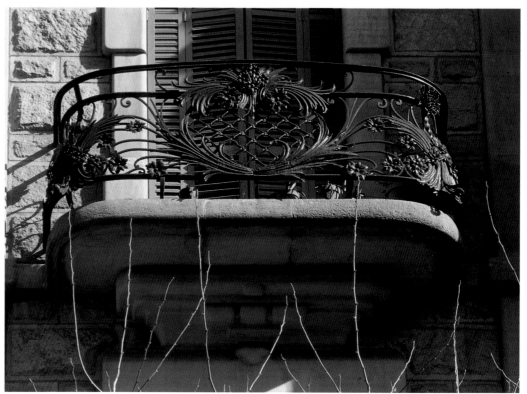

CASA COMALAT

1911
Salvador Valeri i Pupurull (1873-1954),
Architect
Diagonal, 442 / Còrsega, 316

Designed in 1906, it was considered for the City Council prize in 1912. Salvador Valeri was an architect with a small output who produced few buildings in Barcelona, namely:

—1908. Torre Sant Jordi, Carrer de Sant Eudald 7.
—1912. House at Carrer de les Camèlies 5. House at Carrer de les Camèlies 7.
—1913-15. Casa Espona, Carrer del Bisbe Català 8 (mutilated).
—1915. Casa Llaudet, Plaça de la Font Castellana 19.

The Casa Comalat, built towards the end of the Modernista period, was the culmination of ornamentation carried to the extreme. This highly original building is outstanding in having two façades, the front at Diagonal 442 and the back at Còrsega 316 — though it is not the only such building, for the Casa Quadras, now the Museu de Música and mentioned later on in this book, also has two.

The Diagonal façade is a real symphony in stone. Despite the extraordinary quality of the whole front, there are a number of particularly noteworthy features. Two impressive mezzanine balconies, of an originality that is unparalleled in the city and that represent the triumph of the curved line combined with vague evocations of organic elements: one of the most striking aspects is the huge aperture, which recalls to some extent the lower part of Gaudí's Casa Batlló. These two balconies form a spectacular frame for the front door with its creative combination of wood and metal.

Arranged symmetrically across the façade are twelve balconies with voluminous sculptural bases and curvacious wrought-iron railings that are a triumph of that delightful Modernista creation, the whiplash curve.

The double-story oriel window on the principal and first floors is the central dominating feature, though the most decorative and unusual piece is the narrow pinnacle crowning it.

The crest of the façade is formed of two very clearly differentiated parts and is notable precisely for this unprecedented

double composition. The front possesses a sequence of apertures and is profusely decorated. The back is a pinnacle in the shape of a harlequin's cap, composed in this case of bright green ceramic tiles. The overall effect is to give a striking appearance to a façade that would seem to fit in well with the sobriety of Avinguda Diagonal. And I say this because the rear façade is an astonishingly radical creation.

The façade that Valeri designed for the Carrer de Còrsega is imaginatively adapted to an irregularly curved corner. I suspect that this was what provoked the

splendid composition and resulted in the addition of a number of protuberant and even more irregular curves. This being so, the overall result is unusual in its mobility and broken patterns.

I should emphasise the way the shutters are used almost in the manner of a curtain wall. The decoration is at its most florid here, based on the extravagant use of polychrome mosaic forming figures and arabesques. Each floor is underlined by a frieze, and the oval aperture on the parapet is surrounded by a very ornate mosaic decoration that falls away in a large spectacular teardrop.

316

CASA MARCEL·LÍ COSTA

1904
Architect unknown
Diputació, 299

Designed in 1902. This was not a new
building but the Modernista conversion of
the house erected in 1862 by the master
builder Felip Ubach. The four-storey oriel
is dominated, unusually, by the window
panes set in iron frames.

CASA JOSEP I RAMON QUERALTÓ

1907
Josep Plantada i Artigas (?-1925),
Architect
Rambla de Catalunya, 88

Designed in 1906. It is a pity that this beautiful Modernista building, now to be seen in all its splendour thanks to recent restoration, should have had a considerable part of its crest spoilt. It lost a series of pinnacles and the corner turret that gave this delicate part of the façade a more airy, personal and subtle note. This pruning has certainly diminished its attractiveness. On the other hand, the building has not been so greatly affected by the mutilation of the oriel window on the corner and the first floor balcony. The floral sgraffito in maroon on cream confers a sense of unity. Worthy of note is the ornamentation in stone on the base of the balconies. The door is an elegant combination of wood and wrought-iron.

CASA FRANCESC PASTOR

1898
Enric Sagnier i Villavecchia (1858-1931),
Architect
Provença, 258

The plans were completed in 1895 and consisted in the remodelling of the Casa Antoni Marsà, a two-story house built in 1885. Francesc Pastor was a sculptor who worked with Sagnier. Noteworthy features of the façade are the crest inspired in the Neo-Gothic, and the touch of red so characteristic of this architect. The large Modernista figure is the most beautiful of all the compositions in sgraffito to be found in this urban landscape.

CASA ALBERT LLEÓ I MORERA

1906
Lluís Domènech i Montaner (1849-1923),
Architect
Passeig de Gràcia, 35

Designed in 1902. One of the emblematic houses of the Quadrat d'Or, not only because it is a magnificent work by this great architect but also because of the original design of the ground floor — now spoiled — and the fact that it contains one of the most sumptuously decorated flats in the Modernista style on the principal floor. Indeed, I would venture to classify it as a Palau de la Música on a small scale, such is the result of the architect's *horror vacui*. It is interesting to know the names of the artisans who collaborated on such a lavish work: Eusebi Arnau, sculpture; Alfons Juyol, decorative stonework; Antoni Serra i Fiter, ceramics; Rigalt i Granell, stained glass; Escofet, flooring; Mario Maragliano and Lluís Bru, mosaics; Gaspar Homar, furniture and interior decor.

It is therefore not surprising that the house should have been awarded first prize for architecture by the City Council in 1906. The whole façade was an example of exquisite workmanship, particularly on the ground floor. The key pieces at this level were the exceptional sculptures by the great sculptor Eusebi Arnau, consisting of two symmetrical pairs of exceedingly beautiful Modernista females holding large vessels that appeared to be for plants but in fact were not. Their faces and the folds of their tunics were of a sensuality and delicacy that was quite unique. The figures were framed in large apertures, reinforced by two sets of thick double columns in pink marble. The underside of the oriel window was decorated with branching female heads. This marvellous creation was, however, brutally destroyed. And I say brutally, because Josep Gudiol, the internationally renowned art expert who worked in the neighbouring Casa Amatller, told me that he had witnessed those sculptures being broken up with hammers right on the pavement. The heads had been severed from the bodies, and the manager of the shop retrieved them and took them to his summer residence. Dalí discovered what had happened, and fired by his admiration for Modernisme

he purchased them for five thousand pesetas and placed them on the wall of the courtyard of his Theatre-Museum in Figueres.

That outrage is explained by the Noucentistes' hatred of Modernisme, to the extent that the mere sight of the Modernista façades was a physical discomfort. Hence the fact that the renowned architect Ramon Duran Reynals agreed to sign the plans drawn up by a colleague that involved the destruction of the

ground floor and its replacement by the funereal shopfront paid for by Loewe. This shameful result is what we see today. At the time of writing, the City Council has ordered Loewe to remodel this part of the façade, and the work is being carried out under the direction of the architect Oscar Tusquets, who was likewise responsible for replacing the pinnacles and turret that had also been lopped off in the early forties after having been badly damaged when used by snipers in 1937.

CASES JOSEP J. BERTRAND

1904
Enric Sagnier i Villavecchia (1858-1931),
Architect
Balmes, 44-48

Designed in 1902. A number of houses
were produced by this architect for the
same owner. This building is very similar
to the one described on page 24.

CASA MANUEL LLOPIS I BOFILL

1903
Antoni Gallissà i Soqué (1861-1903),
Architect
València, 339 / Bailèn, 113

Designed in 1902. The sgraffito was the work of the architect Josep Maria Jujol. This was without doubt the most ambitious of the buildings designed by Gallissà, an architect of repute who died at an early age. He collaborated closely with Domènech i Montaner and was one of the people responsible for the Cafè-Restaurant being converted after the 1888 Universal Exhibition into a centre for the applied arts that were such an essential feature of Modernisme.

The composition of the façade is of an impressive simplicity, which combined with the almost omnipresent white and the orthogonal pattern of the oriel windows gives the whole building an air of inimitable elegance.

At first sight the eye is drawn to the successful but by no means easy way in which the brick and white are combined. The ground floor is highly original, formed by a rhythmic pattern of segmental arches in brick.

Running the full height of the building are twenty oriel windows set in three blocks — a double block in the centre and the two outer blocks on the corners — each crowned with a turret. The turrets are of an original design and take their inspiration from the Alhambra. This, however, is not the only Neo-Arab note, for the keyhole shapes and the profusion of ceramic ornamentation also point to this influence.

The upper parts of the oriel windows were originally faced in ceramic, but both these and the stained-glass windows suffered irreparable damage from bombing during the Civil War and had to be removed. The overall personality of the façade owes much to the solid symmetry and the white stucco, which accentuates a simplicity that is certainly not often encountered in Modernisme. Gallissà had a self-confessed passion for tiles, of which he was also an avid collector. It is therefore not surprising that he should have employed these to decorate such an outstanding building. He used glazed tiles on the vaulted undersides of the oriel windows and on the quatrefoil panels strategically placed along the ground floor. He designed both the shape and the delicate ornamentation with his own hand, and they were mass-produced by the respected firm of Pujol i Bausis, who then marketed them commercially.

A fundamental feature of the façade is without doubt the sgraffito, the work of the architect Josep Maria Jujol, who had a particular flair for drawing. He designed the fleurons that match the ceramic panels, and others of a circular composition. Jujol chose a single colour, ochre, which stands out subtly against the immaculate white that predominates over the whole façade.

The Farmàcia Arderiu, a delicate example of Modernista cabinet-making that has been carefully preserved, was immediately established on the ground floor.

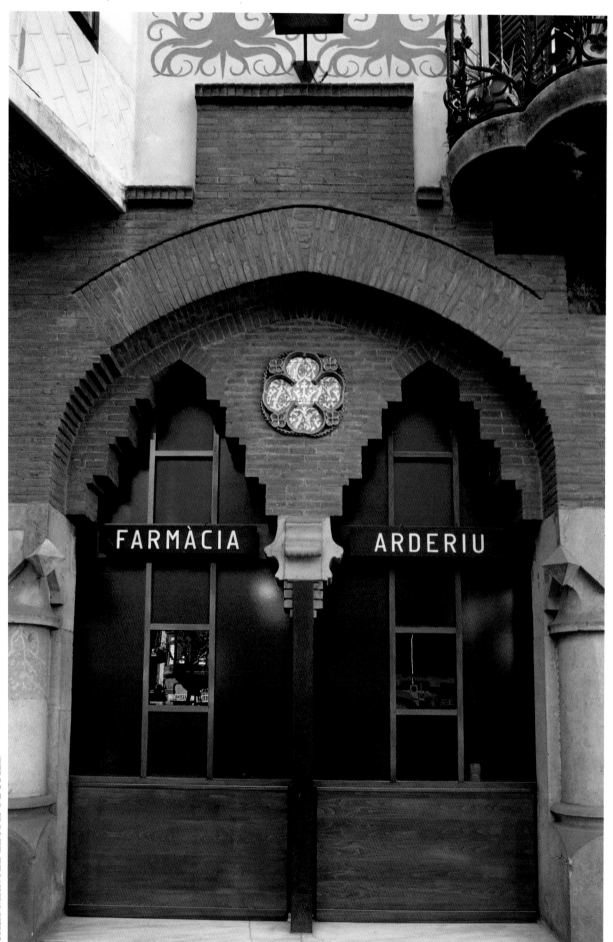

CASA JERONI F. GRANELL

1900
Jeroni F. Granell i Manresa (1867-1931),
Architect
Balmes, 65

A façade adorned with many decorative features. The stone carvings show a sculptural tendency, and those around the windows are of particular interest. The oriel window emphasises the three-dimensional aspect, and the blue sgraffito completes the overall design. All the decoration is based on floral themes, and the delicate wrought-ironwork on the balconies is a triumph of the gestural flourish.

CASA ANDREU CALVET I PINTÓ

1900
Antoni Gaudí i Cornet (1852-1926),
Architect
Casp, 48

Designed in 1898. In 1900 this building won the prize that the City Council started to award that year for distinguished works of architecture. The wrought-ironwork on the façade was by Lluís Badia, and the carpentry by Casas i Bardés.

This was Gaudí's first apartment building in the Eixample. The design is noticeably discreet for an architect with such a strong personality, although he achieved a work of extraordinary quality.

The whole façade is built of blocks of Montjuïc stone. The front door is framed by curious twin columns that can only be interpreted as alluding to the bobbins used in the owner's textile factory. The sculptural form of the oriel window with its rich ornamentation in stone and wrought-iron is one of the most original to be found in the Eixample. The ornate corbel is decorated with various realistic items: a cypress tree, symbolising hospitality; the initial letter "C" of the owner's surname; an olive branch; and the coat-of-arms of Catalonia. On the crest are two horns of plenty. Calvet was an amateur botanist, hence the fact that the highly decorative wrought-ironwork on the oriel window depicts various types of fungi, while a number of flowers are carved in stone.

The windows form a strictly symmetrical pattern and are complemented by two orders of balconies with elegant wrought-iron railings. Two features of note are the tiny, cast-iron balconies at the top of the façade that support the wrought-iron pulleys used for hoisting up furniture.

The parapet with its composition of emphatic curves is, together with the oriel window, the most outstanding feature of the building. On it are three finely carved busts, representing St. Peter the Martyr, in deference to the name of the owner's father; and St. Genesius the Actor and St. Genesius the Notary, the patron saints of Sant Ginés de Vilasar, where the owner of the house was born. Two significant details give the measure of the excellent design that was a distinguishing mark of all the architects of that period. First, the number 48 which

appears on the ground floor in large, flowing, gilded figures and does not comply with the municipal regulation model. For the other detail, one must lift the doorknocker to discover the bug underneath, which was literally squashed every time the knocker was used. The knocker symbolises the cross crushing the symbol of evil. This is Gaudí's most conventional building.

CASA ANDREU CALVET I PINTÓ

CASA AGUSTÍ ANGLORA

1906
Isidre Raventós i Amiguet (1849-1911),
Master Builder
Roger de Llúria, 74

Designed in 1904. An unpretentious façade without any ostentatious features,
typical of the discreet work of a master
builder. Despite its austerity, there is no
lack of ornamental details in stone and the
oriel window is glazed with delicately patterned stained glass.

CASA LLUÍS PÉREZ SAMANILLO

1910
Joan Hervàs i Arizmendi (1851-1912),
Architect
Diagonal, 502-504 / Balmes, 169

Designed in 1909. This is one of the few family mansions remaining in the Quadrat d'Or, and one that has also managed to preserve intact its interior. In 1911 it won the annual prize for architecture awarded at the time by the City Council. On the elegant façade with its well-balanced arrangement of apertures, bow windows on the corners and minimal decorative details, special mention must be made of the large oval window on the Diagonal front. This "goldfish bowl" reminds me of the similar one on the front of the Gran Teatre del Liceu which serves as a balcony for the members of the Cercle del Liceu, for this mansion is now the premises of the Cercle Eqüestre, some of whose members can usually be seen in the room inside.

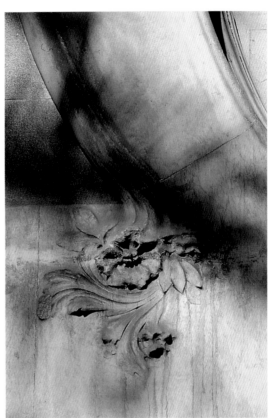

CASA JOSEP THOMAS

1898
Lluís Domènech i Montaner (1848-1923),
Architect
Mallorca, 291-293

Designed in 1895. It was built for the owner of the most important Modernista lithographic, photogravure and printing works, who installed his home and workshop here. It originally consisted of a basement, semi-basement, ground floor, upper story and two towers, forming a delightful family house.

In 1912 the sons of the owner, Eudald and Josep Thomas i Corrons, received permission to enlarge the house, and also obtained the consent of Domènech i Montaner since his building was to be substantially modified.

In fact, three storeys were added. The towers were taken down and used on the crest of the building; one of them had originally been decorated with a stylised, turned stone spire. The plans were drawn up by the architect Francesc Guàrdia i Vial.

A large segmental arch presides over the ground floor. This aperture was protected by a beautifully austere wrought-iron grille in vaguely Modernista style. Since it has been occupied by the firm BD Ediciones de Diseño, the basement can now be admired from the street thanks to a large plate-glass window; the view is indeed gratifying. On the ground floor the original layout of two entrances has been maintained, the main entrance leading directly to the flats, and the secondary entrance to the basement and semi-basement.

The entire façade was built of stone apart from certain ornamental features. The undersides of the balconies, the walls and the friezes on the parapet were covered in polychrome ceramic; the studs dotted over the walls were in metallic glazed ceramic with a heraldic theme.

An outstanding feature is the openwork stone balcony running the width of the principal floor, and the gallery with its carved balustrade and pseudo-Ionic columns decorated with floral motifs.

CASES TOMÀS ROGER

1894
Enric Sagnier i Villavecchia (1858-1931),
Architect
Ausiàs Marc, 37-39

Designed in 1892. The architect still employed very eclectic elements, combining them with ornamental details that already clearly showed the predominance of the curve, that essential mark of Modernisme. Recent restoration has highlighted the formal interest of the sgraffito, perhaps the most striking feature of the façade.

CASA CASIMIR CLAPÉS

1908
Joaquim Bassegoda i Amigó (1854-1938),
Architect
Diputació, 246

Designed in 1907. A particularly spectacular house, not so much for its size — as in the case with the building at Passeig de Gràcia 6-14 — as for the unquestionable artistic quality of the architectural design and the ornamentation.

A typical apartment building where the owner, a member of the wealthy textile bourgeoisie, wanted a house that would proclaim his social standing. It seems that there was considerable competition between house-owners to see who would be noted for having the most beautiful and ostentatious buildings. Needless to say, the architects usually had carte blanche when it came to producing designs.

The whole façade is elegant, richly decorated, solemn and striking. The oriel window is a singular piece, exquisitely worked with the meticulousness and perfection of lace. Its parapet is decorated with a gently modelled relief that represents the textile industry. It has always caught my attention, for the figures are two boys and a young girl chained to a loom — and I say chained because at that time they worked 12 to 14 hours a day without a single day off in the week. A certain discretion would have been more appropriate, but there it is for all the world to see that nobody was ashamed of such merciless exploitation. There is another feature that I also think is worthy of note: the two symmetrical balconies on the top floor. They seem to be literally suspended in space, such was the architect's desire to exaggerate their three-dimensional form. A balcony obviously does not need to project quite so much, and this must therefore be interpreted as an attempt at volume, which until then not been tackled by architects, who — save for a few Modernistes — restricted themselves to a discreet two-dimensionalism.

The crest of the house is also interesting, for it was composed with the aim of highlighting the large niche in which a majestic female figure is seated.

246

CASA MANUEL VERDÚ

1905
Maurici Augé i Robert,
Architect
Rambla de Catalunya, 101

Designed in 1903. The façade is entirely of stone, with a clearly eclectic influence that is particularly obvious in the parapet of historicist inspiration. A detailed figure of a bird adorns the delicate and realist stonework, which also decorates the lintels over the windows and the undersides of the balconies.

CASES PONS AND PASCUAL

1891
Enric Sagnier i Villavecchia (1858-1931),
Architect
Passeig de Gràcia, 2-4

Despite the two houses belonging to members of the same family, Alexandre Pons and Sebastià Pascual, the architect was asked to produce two quite separate establishments within a single overall design. This compositional unity enabled Enric Sagnier to conceive a building that would make a strong statement, for it had the benefit of no less than three façades and two corners. He engaged the services of a number of leading craftsmen: Francesc Pastor for stone-carving, Emili Farrés and Josep Lagarriga for wrought-ironwork, Antoni Rigalt for stained-glass windows. The building belongs to the Neo-Gothic style of Modernisme, particularly noticeable in the window frames and the corner crests. It had been appallingly mutilated, but was carefully restored in the mid-eighties.

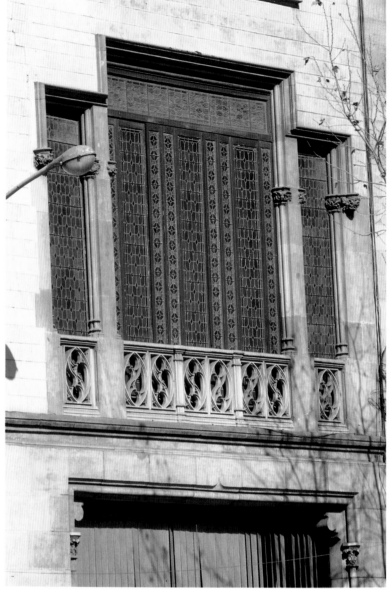

CASA MODEST ANDREU

1904
Telm Fernández i Janot,
Architect
Ali Bei, 3

Designed in 1902. This is an elegant, contained façade built entirely of stone with some intricately worked ornamentation. The decoration is focused mainly on the corbel beneath the oriel window and the well-composed crest with its original balustrade.

CASA DOLORS CALM

1903
Josep Vilaseca i Casanovas (1848-1910),
Architect
Rambla de Catalunya, 54

Designed in 1902 as the remodelling of
the 1878 building by the master builder
Josep Deu. Vilaseca, a distinguished architect and author of the Arc de Triomf
and the picturesque Casa Bruno Quadros
(Rambla/Cardenal Casañas), merely
composed the façade, with its strong personality. The beautiful two-tone sgraffito
is enhanced by the attractive maroon.
The ornate woodwork on the five-story
oriel window was designed by Vilaseca
himself and is embellished with stained-
glass. The sculptural pieces on the cornice were damaged when several extra
floors were added. Especially remark-
able is the underside of the oriel window,
delightfully decorated with sgraffito based on a long-stemmed flower motif.

CASA EVARIST JUNCOSA

1909
Salvador Viñals i Sabaté (1847-1926),
Architect
Rambla de Catalunya, 78

Designed in 1907. The oriel window, and particularly the openwork crest, are the most outstanding features of this Modernista façade, built entirely of stone. Recent restoration has emphasised the overall harmony of the design.

CASA FUSTER

1911
Lluís Domènech i Montaner (1849-1923),
Architect
Passeig de Gràcia, 132

Designed in 1909. The disadvantage of the grid system on which Ildefons Cerdà designed the Eixample is the absence of any focal point at the end of a vista — something that is highly gratifying to the lover of urban landscapes. Unless a large building has a empty space in front of it, such as a square, its visual impact comes from such a vista. If we notice the lack of these scenic effects in the Eixample, the Casa Fuster is perhaps the only example of a building that fulfils such an important mission. It marks the end of what is the most significant street in the Quadrat d'Or: Passeig de Gràcia. The point where the wide Passeig meets the narrow Carrer Gran de Gràcia certainly merited a building of a certain stature. I presume this important planning consideration must have induced the owner, Consol Fabra de Fuster, to engage no less an architect than Lluís Domènech i Montaner, who already enjoyed considerable prestige and respect, for he was then at the height of his career.

The Casa Fuster was his last city building. From the point of view of a personal aesthetic, it can be considered a mature resumé of a number of historical influences. It does not contribute anything new, but within his personal style it is the materialisation of a highly intelligent and effective synthesis of some of his achievements in more emblematic buildings during his intensive career.

It consists of three façades. The two main façades are asymmetrical and arranged around the attractive tower-like oriel window that acts as an effective hinge. It is an audacious piece, suspended in space, for he could not let it continue down to the ground floor and occupy the pavement. The arrangement of apertures has a particular richness and variety of form. The ornamentation is robust, clearly defined and with a notable physical presence on account of its volume. The capitals, for example, are based on compact abstract masses rather than figurative mouldings. The use of two types of marble, pink and white, has led some critics to detect a certain inspiration in Venetian mansions.

The parapet is organised around an elaborate mansard roof, but the impact of the original design, based on an intricately-worked crest in the form of a turret, has been lost.

I think that problems are always of benefit to great designers. And here we have an interesting example. The most imaginative of the three façades is perhaps the third one, giving onto the Carrer de Jesús. The problem was that this street is a very winding one, which prevented the architect from continuing the same three-dimensional pattern he had designed for the Passeig de Gràcia front. Domènech i Montaner found an unusually creative solution: he designed an essentially two-dimensional composition, but without excluding ornamental features, for which he devised the original idea of making incisions on the stone. Such courage paid off, for the result is extremely attractive.

CASA JAUME FORN

1909
Jeroni F. Granell i Manresa (1867-1931),
Architect
Roger de Llúria, 82 / València, 285

Designed in 1904. Jeroni F. Granell, one of the foremost architects of Modernisme and the designer of the delightful façade at Carrer Girona 122, is also labelled by art historians as a pre-Rationalist. In this respect, the house he designed for this corner site is interesting in that it contains elements from quite different aesthetics. The column running up each of the two corners, with its conventional decoration, is a typical feature of eclectic buildings. The overall symmetry and the arrangement of apertures is discreet, allowing the oriel windows adorning the corners to act as the protagonists of the façade. The house was disfigured by the addition of two stories, but I do not know whether Granell had placed any uncompromisingly Modernista ornamentation on the crest. It is in fact hard to find any details that confirm this style.

There are several capitals that perhaps pass somewhat unnoticed. The stone carving on the balconies is in my view one of the few ornamental works in which the *coup de fouet* can be detected within the floral genre. There is also some good floral work in the wrought-iron which, combined with the woodwork, forms the excellent front door.

The most relevant feature is the thoroughly Modernista stained-glass windows, which specialists suspect may be attributed to the well-known firm of Rigalt i Granell.

160

CASES JOAN B. PONS

1909
Joan B. Pons i Trabal (1855-1927),
Architect
Balmes, 81-81 bis

Designed in 1908. Although the two properties belonged to the architect and the
façade was designed as a single unit, the
asymmetry is evident. It is a pity that the
whole front is in such a shabby state. The
day it is restored, we shall be able to admire the delicate colouring of the sgraffito, the highly individual wrought-ironwork on the balconies, the subtle pattern
of the crest and the exceptional stained-
glass windows.

CASA MIQUEL A. FARGAS

1904
Enric Sagnier i Villavecchia (1858-1931),
Architect
Rambla de Catalunya, 47

Sagnier used only stone throughout the façade. The oriel window running virtually the entire height of the house is the distinguishing feature, in addition to the formal composition. The ornamentation is excellent though restrained. The building was originally crowned with a cupola, which was removed when extra floors were added. The additional stories do, however, show a respect for the overall design that is unusual.

CASA RAMON OLLER

1901
Pau Salvat i Espasa (1872-1923),
Architect
Gran Via, 658

Designed in 1900. This was a substantial modification of a house by the distinguished master builder Josep Fontserè. The great craftsman Manuel Ballarín traced his designs in black wrought-iron, which stand out clearly and elegantly against the austere white background. The oriel window is a prominent feature, and the façade is crowned with an overhanging roof.

173

CASA LLORENÇ CAMPRUBÍ

1901
Adolf Ruiz i Casamitjana (1869-1937),
Architect
Casp, 22

Designed in 1900. The elaborate oriel window running almost the full width of the principal floor, with a svelte, intricately worked extension occupying the centre of the first floor, presides over the façade. Two well-sculpted female figures in Modernista style frame the date of the building. The openwork balconies carved in stone and the ornamentation around the windows complete the composition. A notable feature is the crest, where the architect has produced a pattern of alternating parapets and protuberant balconies, all profusely decorated in stone. The front door, carved in wood, is worth noting.

CASES JOSEP J. BERTRAND

1905
Enric Sagnier i Villavecchia (1858-1931),
Architect
Balmes, 50 / Consell de Cent, 274

Designed in 1903. Although this building was constructed for the owner of the houses shown on pages 24 and 98 — Josep J. Bertrand — and despite the fact that red dominates the composition, the outstanding features here are the windows set in the two corners.

CASA MIQUEL SAYRACH

1918
Manuel Sayrach i Carreras (1886-1937),
Architect
Diagonal, 423-425

Designed in 1915. The architect constructed the house for his father, although
he himself lived in it until his death. He
was a wealthy man and produced few
buildings — the house next door in Carrer d'Enric Granados is also his — and
spent his time reflecting on a creative
universe that was both aesthetic and
ethical. His particular world can be better understood by contemplating the entrance halls to the two houses. This was
perhaps the last Modernista building to
be erected in the Eixample; devoid of
decoration, it is a symphony in stone,
gently treated, in which a sensual round-
ness predominates rather than the
whiplash curve. The crest is original in
its conception, with an unusual, artistic
cupola.

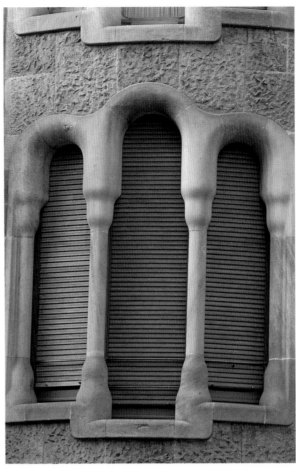

CASA ANTONI AMATLLER

1900
Josep Puig i Cadafalch (1867-1957),
Architect
Passeig de Gràcia, 41

Designed in 1904. In 1901 it won the City Council's prize for the best building constructed in the previous year. It is included in the "Catàleg del Patrimoni". The architect employed leading artists and craftsmen to create a kind of mansion, although the interior retained the layout of an apartment building, for in fact this was not an entirely new building but the remodelling of an existing one designed by the architect Antoni Robert in 1875. The list of those who collaborated on the façade is a long one: Eusebi Arnau, sculpture; Alfons Juyol, stone carving; Esteve Andorrà and Manuel Ballarín, wrought-ironwork; Masriera i Campins, bronzes; Torres Mauri and Fill de J. Pujol, ceramics; Mario Maragliano, mosaics. Puig i Cadafalch was commissioned to design the house by the chocolate manufacturer Antoni Amatller; the art foundation he set up is located on the principal floor. The architect produced the most outstanding building of what is known as his "pink period", which the art critic Alexandre Cirici identifies with his Modernista period.

The front doors are embellished with capitals carved by the famous Modernista sculptor Eusebi Arnau, including one showing St. George slaying the dragon and another depicting a dancing bear.

One of the coats-of-arms is adorned with an almond tree in an allusion to the owner's surname; and almond blossom was used by Alfons Juyol in the leafy decoration of the façade.

The graceful windows along the ground floor have been respected by the various jeweller's shops that have occupied the premises. The upper windows are inspired by those found in Catalan Gothic farmhouses and are decorated with a floral motif. Cirici considered the oriel window to resemble the façade of the chapel of St. George in the Generalitat in the Plaça de Sant Jaume. The elegant balcony is framed in wrought-iron, with lilies supporting the tiles. An important feature is the crest: the stepped gable, with its Northern European air, is in shiny ceramic scattered with fleur-de-lis in relief with a metallic finish. The sgraffito is austere: yellow and white, with a single basic design constantly repeated.

Overall, it is a lesson in historicism and a fine example of asymmetical balance combined with the variations introduced around the tops of the windows.

CASA ENRIC LLORENS

1907
Josep Pérez i Terraza (1852-1907),
Master Builder
Enric Granados, 119 / Còrsega, 261

Designed in 1904. This is a good example of the very high standard of work of the master builders. Josep Pérez i Terraza won the City Council's first prize for the building in 1907. It is a shame that the entire crest has been demolished: the central part consisted of a series of five medallions, with cupolas crowning the corners. The façade is of stone and includes certain eclectic elements, such as the columns at the corners. But the best ornamental details are the sculpted floral motifs.

CASA ROSSEND CAPELLADES

1906
Jeroni F. Granell i Manresa (1867-1931),
Architect
Bailèn, 126

Designed in 1904. Interesting ornamental
stone carving with beautiful Modernista
female heads. The most outstanding feature is the top floor in subtly patterned
ceramic tiles.

CASA SOCIETAT TORRES GERMANS

1908
Jaume Torres i Grau (1879-1945),
Architect
Aribau, 178 / Aribau, 180 / París, 180

Designed in 1906. A strange building, for despite the fact that the owner, the architect and the business were one and the same, the façade was designed in three distinct parts, that is to say, the two corners and the central section. While the central part is eclectic and decorated with sgraffito on the basis of straight lines, the sides are markedly Modernista, composed in stone with a predominance of curves.

CASES FRANCESC LALANNE

1910
Arnau Calvet i Peyronill (1875-1956),
Architect
Provença, 324-326

These two houses were designed in 1907. The delicate and gestural wrought-iron-work on the balconies, the sculptural stone parapet over the oriel window, the consols and the carving over the windows on the top floor are the most noteworthy features of a discreet, well-balanced façade.

CASA PERE SERRA I PONS

1908
Josep Puig i Cadafalch (1867-1957),
Architect
Rambla de Catalunya, 126

Designed in 1903. A single-family house with the appearance of a mansion, although its present external aspect has been the inevitable result of a series of vicissitudes of various kinds. It was presented for the Council's annual prize in 1908, but was rejected on account of not having been entirely finished. And it never was entirely finished. Indeed, in 1908 it ceased to be a private house and was turned into a convent school. During the Civil War it was the headquarters of the Ministry of Health, after which the nuns reopened their school and it was then decided to enlarge the building. A different architect was commissioned for the job, and the work was carried out between 1943 and 1945. In 1969 the nuns started to negotiate the sale of the building, and a few years later it was on the point of being demolished, though such an aberration was eventually averted. Another problem arose, however, once the house had been saved: the remodelling of the building to house the Diputació de Barcelona meant demolishing the additions, which led to an outburst of criticism that was in my view entirely unreasoned.

It seems right that the team of architects Federico Correa/Alfonso Milà should have strictly respected the work of Puig i Cadafalch, eliminating all spurious additions and daring to marry this structure to a curtain wall, for proximity is always good between buildings of a high standard of design.

Puig i Cadafalch carried out an exercise in history combined with nostalgia: he recreated the Palau Gralla, one of the few Renaissance buildings in the city, which had disappeared in the middle of the nineteenth century under the pickaxes wielded by the speculators. The front door and the ornamentation on the windows are a fairly faithful reconstruction, for this was his personal way of paying tribute. The distinguished Modernista sculptor Eusebi Arnau and the renowned stone-carver Alfons Juyol, both of whom habitually collaborated with the architect, were involved in the work. There are also a number of medallions and coats-of-arms which bear a clear allusion to the name of the owner in the form of a saw. A tower of mediaeval inspiration acts as a hinge between the two asymmetrical wings. The façade is entirely of stone, and is crowned with an overhanging roof. On the main door, with its air of belonging to another age, the door-knocker is a prominent feature — although it is not the original one, which was stolen. Puig i Cadafalch carried his tribute to the past to such an extreme that he designed with his own hand a Gothic door-knocker, which disappeared one night during the restoration work carried out in the mid-eighties, and despite intense investigations has never been found.

CASA PERE SERRA I PONS

CASA VERDÚ

1903
Maurici Augé i Robert,
Master Builder
València, 250

Exceptionally fine stonework both on the
undersides of the balconies and around
the windows. Particularly outstanding is
the carving of the Modernista female
heads.

CASA VÍDUA MARFÀ

1905
Manuel Comas i Thos (1855-1914),
Architect
Passeig de Gràcia, 66 / València, 274

Designed in 1904. Despite the fact that Modernisme was well advanced by then and had already reached its peak some years earlier, the architect was still influenced by historicism. Although the building is clearly of neo-mediaeval inspiration, he employed a decidedly personal language. The fact of it being on a corner site on the splendid Passeig de Gràcia — its unusual width shows off the buildings to gratifying advantage — enabled Comas to design a magnificent, grandiose house, for the left-hand façade is of a considerable size. The principal virtue of this building is its elegance combined with sobriety. In this respect, two of its best features are the main entrance and the oriel window, which complement and enhance each other. The doorway is one of the most beautiful in the Eixample after the Pedrera; the three arches forming the entrance — the latter interesting and sumptuous in concept rather than in size — constitute a highly original and imposing frame. The arcaded balcony above is embellished with fine stone carvings — gargoyles, capitals, etc. — by that most renowned ornamental stone-carver of the period, Alfons Juyol.

PALAU BARÓ DE QUADRAS

1906
Josep Puig i Cadafalch (1867-1957),
Architect
Diagonal, 373 / Roselló, 279

Designed in 1904. Collaborators: Eusebi Arnau, sculptor; Alfons Juyol, ornamental stonework; Manuel Ballarín, wrought-ironwork. Baron Manuel de Quadras once again commissioned this outstanding architect to design a building for him. And I say once again, for he had already engaged him to refurbish the old family mansion north of Barcelona between Hostalric and Maçanet de la Selva. The Baron was delighted with the work carried out there, and as soon as it was completed he suggested that the architect design his Barcelona residence. Puig i Cadafalch found himself having to remodel an existing house. This was quite customary in the Eixample, and a practice that all the great architects accepted. What is important is to underline the skill with which those masters not only managed to deal with the demands of the owners but also to erect true works of art despite having their hands tied.

The Diagonal façade gives the building the appearance of a family mansion, although this was not at all the case, as can clearly be seen from the back of the house on Carrer Roselló. Although the site was nothing special in itself, for it is only twelve metres wide, the architect made the best of it and produced an attractive building devoid of ostentation. The main façade was built entirely of stone, which gives it a sombre appearance. The touch of distinction was conferred by the sculptor Eusebi Arnau and the ornamental stone-worker Alfons Juyol, who produced a lavish and extremely fine ornamentation. The most notable accomplishment is the oriel window composed of a series of segmental arches supported on Aztec imposts, which boasts a profusion of filigree stonework that is without precedent in Barcelona. Although it is difficult to pick out any one detail of this sumptuous façade, the masterpiece is the figure of St. George slaying the dragon, carved by Arnau, who always took advantage of the slightest opportunity to depict this legendary fight. Both figures were aligned on the left-hand corner, mounted one above

the other in an exaggeratedly vertical position dictated by the space chosen. On the second floor are four Gothic windows, also richly decorated. The top floor contains an arcaded gallery. The crest is particularly original, for Puig i Cadafalch chose a dark-coloured roof, steeply pitched and with a wide overhang, with dormer windows, wooden gables of Alsatian inspiration and ornamentation on the basis of glazed tiles, perhaps because he felt that anything more spectacular would divert attention from the oriel window. In addition to all this, the façade is embellished with all manner of ornate details such as heraldic emblems, wreathes,

garlands, medallions and busts. Ballarín produced an attractive and imposing wrought-iron and glass front door. On the back of the building the charming, colourful floral sgraffito is concentrated on the crest and the various friezes. What is most striking about the prominent four-story oriel window — three bays wide on the principal floor — is that a prosaic ochre-coloured shutter forms the most conspicuous part of the façade. The door in wrought-iron and glass was also designed by Ballarín.

The building now houses the Music Museum and was painstakingly restored in 1988.

CASA BALDOMER ROVIRA

1900
Andreu Audet i Puig (1868-1938),
Architect
Rosselló, 247

Designed in 1899. An eclectic building with a number of Modernista ornamental details. Interesting balconies in open stonework. The crest is rather original, being based on a series of cupolas rather than a single dome. The most interesting aspect of this façade, to my mind, is its paternity, for it is the only apartment building designed by the architect Andreu Audet, who was responsible for that historical, emblematic edifice — the Hotel Colón — that occupied one of the most central points of the city: the corner of Plaça de Catalunya and Passeig de Gràcia.

CASA JOAN COMA

1907
Enric Sagnier i Villavecchia (1858-1931),
Architect
Passeig de Gràcia, 74

Designed in 1904. Despite being a conversion of a house built in 1882, Sagnier not only composed the façade but also made substantial changes to a considerable part of the interior. This time the architect rejected the use of colour and employed stone alone to achieve an elegant, symmetrical front with no concession to ornament. The wrought-iron-work on the balconies shows not the least trace of Modernisme, as if not wanting to steal the limelight from the exquisitely worked stone balustrades. The four balconies on the principal floor and the balcony attractively crowning the oriel window — unusual in its austerity — were carved with a delicacy that only the Modernistes were able to attain. One cannot but admire the balance between the open stonework in the centre and the subtle, evocative relief work around it. The entire façade also benefits from a well-conceived undulating line. The upper part is uncluttered and simple, allowing attention to be focused on the ornamental details in the centre; and the whole is crowned with a discreet, gently curving cornice.

CASA JERONI F. GRANELL

1903
Jeroni F. Granell i Manresa (1867-1931),
Architect
Girona, 122

Designed in 1901. One of the most orderly and thoroughly Modernista houses in the Quadrat d'Or. Not for nothing was Granell considered a master of this style. The two-tone sgraffito has the quality of a carpet laid vertically and harmonizes perfectly with the subtle reliefs in stone that add a decorative touch very typical of Modernisme. There is nothing ostentatious about the façade — not even the principal floor, which is usually the most highly decorated since it is generally where the owner resides. The front door combines wood with empty spaces that also fulfil an ornamental role. The restoration of this house won the City of Barcelona Prize. The mauve shutters are unique in the Eixample, and the precise tone was given to the architect in charge of the cleaning by some French tenants who, despite their advancing age, clearly remembered the original colour of the house; to avoid any misunderstanding when it came to describing it, they handed him a particular orchid as a sample.

CASA AMADEU MARISTANY

1905
Bonaventura Bassegoda i Amigó (1862-1940),
Architect
Mallorca, 273

Designed in 1902. This house is one of two occupying the site of the Teatre Líric, the famous theatre built by the banker Evaristo Arnús. When it was unfortunately demolished — it was perhaps the most luxuriously appointed theatre after the Liceu — his heirs sold the site to Amadeu Maristany, who commissioned the architect Bonaventura Bassegoda i Amigó to design two separate apartment buildings. This house has been mistakenly attributed to Lluís Domènech i Montaner. The façade is eclectic, and decidedly sober in tone despite the abundance of ornamental details. The oriel window is of wrought-iron, embellished with an interesting decorative frieze. The straight line governs the overall design, including the balconies. The front door is elegant and austere.

CASA FRANCESC CAIRÓ

1907
Domènech Boada i Piera (1866-1947),
Architect
Enric Granados, 106

Designed in 1906. An elegant façade composed on the basis of stone, exquisitely sculpted, particularly on the principal floor. The volume of the balconies denotes a desire to reach out spectacularly into space. The elegant front door is framed in a dramatic curve.

CASA PERE MILÀ I CAMPS

1910
Antoni Gaudí i Cornet (1852-1926),
Architect
Passeig de Gràcia, 92

Designed in 1905. It was not considered for the municipal prize as it had not been fully completed. A number of people collaborated on the façade: Josep Maria Jujol, architect; Germans Badia, wrought-ironworkers; Mañach, founder; Josep Bayò, builder; Joan Beltran, plasterer.
The construction of "La Pedrera" (the stone quarry), as it is popularly known by the people of Barcelona, meant the demolition of the small Hotel Ferrer-Vidal. The building consists of a basement, semi-basement, ground floor, five upper floors and two penthouses. Its total volume is 4,000 cubic metres, more than was permitted under planning regulations. As soon as the building was finished, a local government official immediately reported this fact, and it was feared that the Council would order the top to be lopped off; good sense prevailed, however, and it was duly approved in view of the fact that it was such a unique work of architecture.
What Gaudí had in fact designed was a gigantic sculpture in which the curve held sway — as demanded by Modernisme — and not a single straight line was employed, not even inside the building. The blocks of Garraf stone were carved in a way that gives the impression of a rich *non finito* similar to that practised by Michelangelo. The windows in the semi-basement were protected with wrought-iron grilles, which were removed when the shops were installed; only two remain, flanking the main entrance.
The building represents a mountain, with its undergrowth and hollows, topped with a stone frieze — inspired, I believe, by the mountain of Sant Sadurní near the village of Gallifa in the Vallès, where the ceramicist Llorens Artigas later went to live — and a cloud, which should have been crowned with an enormous statue of Our Lady in gilded bronze, modelled by Carles Mani. Luckily, this distinctly prosaic statue of little artistic merit was never produced because of Milà's refusal to see the model. On the cornice Gaudí inscribed the pious words *Ave-gratia-M-plena-Dominus-tecum*. Below the "M"

was a sculpted bud — the mystic rose. The iron railings on the balconies are the gestural, spontaneous work of the architect Jujol, the genius who also designed the abstract decoration on the façade of the Casa Batlló and on the seats in the Park Güell. When Pau Gargallo and Julio González first saw these railings, they realised the possibilities of iron sculpture, and thus both passed into the universal history of sculpture as the first sculptors to have used this material.
The roof is a worthy crown to the building. The ventilators, hatches and chimneys form an artistic garden that is astonishing in its variety and its avant-garde forms, which had already been hinted at on the roof of Gaudí's Palau Güell.
"La Pedrera" is one of the most imaginative, avant-garde and artistic buildings in the entire history of architecture. I think it is a mistake to classify it as Modernista, for it is undoubtedly a forerunner of the Expressionism that was to make its appearance shortly afterwards.

CASA RAMON CASAS

1899
Antoni Rovira i Rabassa (1845-1919),
Architect
Passeig de Gràcia, 96

Designed in 1898. This apartment building was built by Antoni Rovira for the painter Ramon Casas, who then moved in to live there. It is curious to note how such a large number of the leading exponents of Modernisme belonged to the upper middle classes; this certainly enabled them to live comfortably and to devote themselves entirely to art. Ramon Casas came from a family that was well off, as were those of Rusiñol and Riquer, to name but a couple of examples.

The façade is of finely-worked stone of a single type. The overall composition is not particularly striking, but shows the architect's efforts to achieve a high degree of elegance and austerity combined with a certain amount of ornamentation. The most outstanding feature, strangely enough, is the top floor with its row of small windows. The crest is the repetition of a single, rather prosaic, decorative motif.

Antoni Rovira, who also designed the house next door at number 94, engaged the services of craftsmen of considerable repute: the interior decorator Josep Pascó for Ramon Casas's own flat, the Flinch brothers for the wrought-ironwork, and Josep Orriols for the ceramics, whose work can still be admired today in Vinçon, the shop on the ground floor.

I do not know who was responsible for the ornamental stonework on the façade, but he was clearly a magnificent craftsman. The balconies are one of the most intricately carved elements, the one on the principal floor being the most impressive. The door is one of the best in the Quadrat d'Or. Although it is in no way spectacular or particularly eye-catching, its restrained design reveals a series of highly sensitive and exquisitely drawn details executed with a rare degree of perfection. In addition, the metalwork forms a lucid counterpoint to the wood and wrought-iron.

CASA MANUEL MALAGRIDA

1908
Joaquim Codina i Matalí (?-1910),
Architect
Passeig de Gràcia, 27

Designed in 1905. Notable for the architect's attempt to give it the appearance of a mansion — despite the fact that it is an apartment building — which in times past was the most characteristic type of building in Passeig de Gràcia, the main artery of the Quadrat d'Or. However, this intention is more obvious in the crest than in the composition of the rest of the façade. In fact, the two dormer windows on the top floor leading the eye to the central dome have a markedly French air. The wrought-ironwork that forms the base of the weather vane and lightning conductor is among the most artistically creative in the entire city. In this respect, it is interesting to note that it gave rise to the very first work done by Antoni Clavé as a young lad. He had just started working at Tolosa, the commercial painters, and was allocated the task of giving a coat of red lead to the ironwork. The inexperienced youth had an attack of vertigo. It should be noted that the original colour was gold, rather than the present-day black.

CASA ÀNGEL BATLLÓ

1896
Josep Vilaseca i Casanovas (1848-1910),
Architect
Mallorca, 253-257

Designed in 1891. The owner had divided the site into three properties but the architect produced a unified design, although each house had its own entrance and staircase. The recent restoration of one of them clearly demonstrated the division of the estate. This was the largest apartment building produced by Vilaseca. The attractive projecting balconies, with their finely worked stone corbels, seem to defy gravity. The delightfully engraved ornamental details are subtle but effective, and the interesting front door is basically of wood. The most spectacular feature is the composition of the top floor and crest, with its strong arcaded pattern and decorative motifs.

CASES ANTONI ROCAMORA

1917
Joaquim Bassegoda i Amigó (1854-1938),
Architect
Passeig de Gràcia, 6-14

Designed in 1914. This was one of the last Modernista constructions, for a number of architectural historians all cite this date as marking the end of the style. Joaquim Bassegoda, noted member of a prestigious family of architects, produced a singular building of imposing size, exceeded only in the Quadrat d'Or by the one popularly known as the Casa de les Punxes by Josep Puig i Cadafalch, the only completely detached building in the Eixample. Bassegoda wished to emphasise the importance of the property and the site with a unified design — not a very frequent occurrence. The style is eloquent and grandiose, elegant and self-assured, without affectation, and with a certain Gothic touch. He relied for effect on the oriels, the balanced pattern of windows, the pinnacles and the cupolas, rather than resorting to ornamentation and the applied arts.

CASA TERRADES

1905
Josep Puig i Cadafalch (1867-1957),
Architect
Diagonal, 416-420

This irregular-shaped site was acquired by Angela Brutau, vídua de Terrades, who commissioned Puig i Cadafalch to design a unified building divided into three separate houses each with its own individual entrance and staircase — one for each of her daughters, Angela, Josefa and Rosa.

Here we have the very best example of an apartment building that, in addition to consisting of various units, is imbued with the air of not just a family mansion but a veritable castle. The architect confirmed his professional skill and once again produced a building that rose to the occasion. The Casa Terrades — or Casa de les Punxes — is the most outstanding and coherent of all the buildings in the Eixample that were originally conceived as detached units, for the general rule was to build between party walls — in other words, to fill a gap in a terraced row.

Puig i Cadafalch, as usual, surrounded himself with accredited craftsmen such as Alfons Juyol for ornamental stonework, Manuel Ballarín for wrought-ironwork, and Masriera i Campins for metalwork. Although almost all of the essential ornamentation was in Calafell stone, there were a number of decorative details in ceramic.

One of the tiled panels was composed as a sundial, inscribed with the legend *Numquam te crastina fallet hora.*

Another panel was to cause an outburst of criticism on account of its frankly political statement. The figure of the legendary St. George, patron saint of Catalonia, is represented in the traditional attitude of slaying the dragon; it was adorned with the following legend: *Sant patrò de Catalunya torneu-nos la llibertat* (Patron saint of Catalonia give us back our freedom). Such a claim was not well received in non-nationalist sectors, and it led to all sorts of pressures to have it removed. It is not surprising, therefore, that the professional demagogue Lerroux should have gone to the point of publishing an article under the title of "Separatismo y Arquitectura" in *El Progreso* of 10th November 1907, in which he accused the architect of a "crime against the nation". God help us. In actual fact, the controversial legend had been placed on the crest of the building, that is to say, where hardly anybody could read it. In the end it was left as it was and the whole affair subsided into nothing.

The predominant material in the building is red brick, which played a leading role in Modernista architecture, despite the fact that not a few architects were against it because they considered it unrepresentative of Catalan architecture. Puig i Cadafalch used stone only in the ornamentation.

The overall style of the building is markedly mediaeval and Northern European, much the same as the crest of the Casa Amatller in Passeig de Gràcia. Its outstanding features are the bay windows, the slim towers, the delicate ornamental work around the balconies, and the subtle yet emphatic wrought-ironwork.

SCULPTURAL ORIEL WINDOWS

In the Gothic era, the window marked the territory from which those in power could observe the street in which the mass of people lived permanently. If at that time it implied a certain social category and distancing, the oriel window was later to perfect such a situation, although with time it became a feature reduced to strictly aesthetic qualities while still preserving a certain residual social function. One of the last latticed windows in Barcelona can be seen at number 21 Carrer de Montcada, a Gothic mansion. The oldest oriel in wood is at the top of the new Palau Episcopal in the Plaça Nova, alongside one of the Roman towers.

In the walled city of Barcelona there was so little space in which to build new houses that people resorted to all manner of devices for enlarging their homes so that more people could be fitted in. This was the origin of the projecting façades and of a dangerous proliferation of oriel windws. And I say dangerous, because in those very narrow streets they threatened to take up the little remaining free space. The City Council decided to prohibit their construction on the grounds that they hindered the passage of the air that was "so good for people's health". When the walls were eventually demolished and the city was able to expand over the immense area of the Eixample, the oriel soon flourished again. It was then no longer a means of gaining space but an architectural feature of the first order designed to embellish the façade. For an oriel window is an element of considerable volume, suspended in space, with sculptural projections that allow the architect to give free rein to his artistic rather than constructional talents. It can either be limited to a single aperture, like a jewel encrusted on the façade of the building, or else can run vertically over several storeys or horizontally along one floor.

The oriel is a manifestation of the desire to carry the traditional two-dimensional façade into a third dimension, and at times can attain a truly theatrical grandeur.

The Eixample possesses the widest imaginable variety of oriels. All the different types are well represented, not only in

Gran de Gràcia, 7

stone but also in iron, and with a preponderance of stained glass.

During the Modernista period and right up until the early fifties, the oriel window was a distinguished and privileged place. Ladies used it as a place to sit, but especially as a perfect viewpoint from which to watch the goings-on in the street below and keep an eye on the social life of the neighbourhood. Hence the fact that it was popularly known as "a parked car", conjuring up a vivid and accurate image. But when traffic began to increase to the point where it became infernal, the oriel windows were gradually vacated and most were closed off or turned into a lifeless storeroom. *Sic transit...* A great pity indeed.

Rambla de Catalunya, 112 / Rosselló, 243-245

Rambla de Catalunya, 23

Mallorca, 308

284

Balmes, 54

Rambla de Catalunya, 61 / Aragón, 262

Mallorca, 264

Balmes, 83

València, 293

Balmes, 85

287

Rambla de Catalunya, 92-94

Aribau, 175

Provença, 131

Bruc, 38 / Casp, 54

A WEALTH OF ORNAMENTAL DETAIL

Every time I look closely at the ornamental details on a façade, I inevitably think of photography. For photography is an art that operates on the basis of subtraction, whereas painting, for example, operates by addition. Photography is therefore the most appropriate vehicle for showing up all the fascinating details. It eliminates all superfluities, thus isolating and concentrating the eye on the central theme. Faced with the magnificent ornamentation on many façades, the unaccustomed or inexperienced viewer would quite certainly find himself mesmerized by such an abundance of themes and would notice only a very few details.

The landscape of Barcelona has an unsuspected wealth of ornament. The residents themselves discover it precisely by browsing through illustrated books such as this one. Some façades require meticulous, systematic observation, for the architect made the most of every single corner by filling each one with decorative elements. And for this he employed a variety of artistic methods, materials and genres. Thus we find sculptural plasterwork, ceramic tiles, wrought-iron, metalwork, etc.

The practice of adorning façades with female figures is perhaps the most ancient, for it has been used since the Middle Ages to indicate brothels. Some still remain, though very few; the best-known is the one that gave its name to the entire building: La Carassa. Most frequently encountered in the Eixample are human heads, exotic or otherwise, Modernista ladies or American Indian warriors. There are also numerous animals. In this respect, the most outstanding is the Casa dels Cargols on the corner of Carrer de Entença and Carrer de Tamarit. The entire façade is composed of a single ornamental motif — a snail — represented in a variety of ways. The reason for this is that the owner of the property went out into the fields one day to gather snails and came upon a hoard of gold coins; with his new-found wealth he built the house and added a personal tribute in gratitude to the snails.

Any subject can serve for ornamental purposes. Door-knockers can be designed as a simple functional item for calling

Rambla de Catalunya, 21

the residents — one knock per floor followed by short taps for each door — but also as a small work of art to show off the craftsman's skill. The same goes for the lamps, some of which are real sculptures, as for example the one on the Farmàcia Viladot at number 40 Ronda de Sant Pere.

The façades in the Eixample are a landscape in which however often and carefully we look we will discover some delightful new detail every time.

Rambla de Catalunya, 21

Provença, 332

Rambla de Catalunya, 21

València, 223

Girona, 132

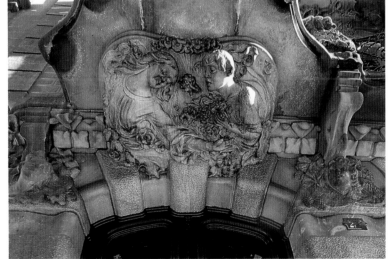

Ausiàs Marc, 22

Girona, 120

Rambla de Catalunya, 102 / Provença, 241

Aribau, 141 / Còrsega, 241

Rambla de Catalunya, 17

Passeig de Colom, 11

Ausiàs Marc, 31

Provença, 332

Rambla de Catalunya, 86 / Mallorca, 248

Roger de Llúria / Plaça Urquinaona

ORNATE STONE AND WROUGHT-IRON BALCONIES

The records tell us that it was around 1662 that the first balcony was projected into space on the city wall, opposite the Col·legi de Betlem in the Rambles; for until then only windows existed.

The oldest existing balcony is the one on the corner of Carrer de Assahonadors and Carrer de Montcada. Among those built on wooden beams is the one at number 4 Carrer de Corders.

In those days the undersides of the balconies were decorated with tiles, most of which were divided diagonally into two colours, with green and cream being the almost inevitable combination. This tiling, to my mind, is a good solution, for not only is it pleasing to the eye but it also helps to keep the underside in better condition. Those early balconies were protected by simple railings in some quite unimaginative pattern, but which in the future were to become a decorative feature of the first order.

Between 1845 and 1850, a good number of public buildings began to have their iron railings replaced by stone or marble balustrades, as was the case with the City Hall, Banco de Barcelona, Gran Teatre del Liceu, Fonda Quatre Nacions and Can Tresserra.

Shortly afterwards came the fashion for cast iron, and despite the fact that the same few models were generally repeated all over the place, on some houses notable works of a highly individual nature were produced.

But it was not until the eruption of Modernisme that the real works of art appeared. Catalonia was a country of wrought-ironworkers, and this once again became patently obvious when the architects not only gave them permission to demonstrate their skill but also encouraged their individualism. I suspect, too, that the very nature of the Eixample led to that fever to produce something different. For the width of the streets and pavements allowed passers-by to view this unexpected landscape from a sufficient distance. The narrow, winding streets of the old city would never have done justice to such a proliferation of imaginative façades.

The wrought-iron railings and stone balustrades were an embellishment that

Passeig de Gràcia, 75 / Mallorca, 275

was a delight to behold. In only a few years the sensual but monotonous turned baluster had given way to the whiplash curve and the luxuriant floral pattern. The principal floor was the story in which the greatest oppulence was concentrated, not so much because it was where the owner lived as because, being occupied by a single flat, it could have a balcony running across several windows, with the greater artistic scope that this provided. There are stone balustrades that look like the finest lacework; and there are wrought-iron balconies that look like pieces of Modernista jewellery. And yet, I feel that when it comes to assessing the artistic qualities and features of a façade, the balconies unfortunately receive little attention or are even unjustly ignored.

Balmes, 85-87

Aribau, 160 / Còrsega, 230

Rambla de Catalunya, 17

Enric Granados

Pau Claris, 154-156

Rambla de Catalunya, 92-94

Balmes, 158-160

ORNATE STONE AND WROUGHT-IRON BALCONIES

Rambla de Catalunya, 74 / València, 239

Girona, 113

Balmes, 54

302

Rosselló, 293

València, 241

Ausiàs Marc, 20

Rambla de Catalunya, 103

Passeig de Gràcia, 113

IMPOSING DOORS

The front door of a Modernista building is more functional than spectactular, although this functional nature in no way detracts from its quality; if anything, it adds to it.

Whereas the façade was designed to draw attention, the door fulfilled the simple function of permitting entry to the building. Any lavish ornamental detail was reserved, for example, for the immediate interior — the entrance hall. It is worthwhile giving some attention to entrance halls, for they are an anteroom to the splendid decoration to be found on the principle floor, the story that was always occupied by the owner of the property.

The door frame was generally used by decorative stoneworkers — Juyol in particular — as an opportunity to run riot with their chisels. There are some lintels that are truly spectacular. Among those photographed here, the most intricately worked is the door of Casa Cabot, in Carrer de Roger de Llúria 8-10, the work of the sculptors Vives and Alavedra. Other lintels were sculpted by artists of the category of Eusebi Arnau; and there are yet others in which an enormous fleuron serves as a link with the base of the balcony or oriel window.

There is one work of art that I have really fallen in love with. It is the two pine trees framing the front door of the Casa Antònia Burés at Ausiàs Marc 42-46. They are a surprising pair of trees, of a painstakingly-executed realism, to the point that one can even count the number of pine-cones on them. In all the Modernista buildings in Barcelona there is only one work of greater excellence, and that is the emotively outlined tree modelled by Dídac Massana i Majò, the artist responsible for a large part of the proscenium arch of the Palau de la Música Catalana (for the cavalcade of the Walkyrie was designed by the great Pau Gargallo). The legend grew up that the pine trees owed their origin to the fact that the surname of the architect who had designed the house was Pi; however, recent research published in 1990 informs us that the author was the architect Juli Batllevell i Arús.

Front doors were almost always made of wood, occasionally embellished with

Passeig de Gràcia, 113

wrought-iron trimmings. They were generally distinguished by being solid and austere. Engravings, incisions, mouldings, knockers of varying degrees of artistic quality — these were some of the ornamental details that we can still admire today.

In the early eighties, however, it became the fashion to replace these exquisite wooden doors with appalling glass and aluminium structures of the most tasteless, ordinary kind. This was alleged to be due to the fact that the porters or concièrges were increasingly being replaced by entryphones, and the opening and closing mechanism — so it was said — could not cope with those massive wooden doors; in addition, the glass panels were more practical in that they prevented the en-

trance hall from being enveloped in darkness as a result of the doors being permanently shut, with the consequent risk of muggings. Pure fabrication. At any rate, the owners began to get rid of the doors, and a number of important pieces thus disappeared — or, rather, were sold to foreign antique dealers. Until reason finally prevailed.

The lintel was usually the spot selected for carving in relief the interlinked initials of the owner of the building.

Until the time when it became compulsory to have a porter in every house — March 1908 — the door also had its social language: one leaf closed would signal the death of one of the residents.

Certainly, an imposing door adds a definite touch of quality to a façade.

Roger de Llúria, 8-14

Passeig de Colom, 11

Ausiàs Marc, 46

Provença, 185

Ausiàs Marc, 22

Balmes, 109

Girona, 46

Rambla de Catalunya, 27

Casp, 45

París, 204

Rambla de Catalunya / Mallorca

CRESTS, FINIALS AND CUPOLAS

A distinguishing mark of Barcelona is its diversity. If we compare its landscape with that of other Western cities, this diversity becomes even more apparent, for the characteristic panorama perceived by a person strolling around London or Paris or Berlin is one of uniformity, with here and there a palace or a large building. Given this fact, the reaction of the French politician Clemenceau, when he visited Barcelona, is not surprising. He got off the train at Passeig de Gràcia-Aragó, climbed into a cab, and asked to be driven around the district. But as soon as he had gone two or three blocks along Barcelona's grandest avenue, he ordered the driver to turn round; he could not stand the sight of such architectural diversity, which quite likely he found anarchic and outrageous.

This particular characteristic occurs in all its magnificence in the Eixample. It is understandable, for here the bourgeoisie found land on which they could build as much as they could afford; in addition, it was a mark of social standing to build a large house, if possible of a highly individual design, and in this they vied with each other. But what also contributed decisively was the fact that the golden age of the Eixample should have coincided with an architectural style such as Modernisme. Had it been Noucentisme, for example, things would have been very different.

If the façade allows the architect the most artistic freedom — for the interior has to fulfil certain functional obligations — it is on the crest that he can let his imagination really run wild.

It is a pity that pedestrians generally tend to go around with their eyes cast down, or at best only look up as far as the principal floor. One must walk the Eixample with one's head in the air so as not to miss one of the city's most pleasing landscapes.

Luckily the use of the French-style mansard roof, brought over by Próspero Verboom when he designed the Governor's palace in what is now the Parc de la Ciutadella in 1748, did not take root here. The mansard is anonymous, and is aesthetically more appropriate to cold climates.

Rambla de Catalunya, 17

In general, the great Modernista façades benefitted from a striking crest, despite the fact that the traditional Barcelona roof, the *terrat*, dating back to the time of Jaume I, is flat. The horizontal line of a flat roof edged with a balustrade does not give room for much artistic licence; but without forfeiting the functional nature of these roofs, the Modernista architects managed to produce some particularly theatrical crests and parapets.

The buildings designed by Gaudí are perhaps the most outstanding, but one is taken aback to come across a rather ordinary house crowned with no less than a butterfly in brilliantly coloured glazed ceramic. I have to admit to being captivated by this, both because of the sheer excellence of the design and because it appears so unexpectedly on a very commonplace building — which goes to show how deeply rooted Modernisme was in this district. It is worth paying a visit to the Carrer de Llançà, just where it joins Gran Via: the Casa Faiol, nicknamed the Casa de la Papallona because of the butterfly, is the work of Josep Graner.

The cupolas are another feature that serves to embellish the crests. They come in many styles, designed for many purposes. Although the most outstanding ones are on the more important buildings, there are plenty of others to be seen around the area.

For an architect, the crest is the icing on the cake.

Passeig de Sant Joan, 6

Diagonal, 436

Passeig de Sant Joan, 84 bis

Diagonal, 520

València, 293

Diagonal, 478

Ausiàs Marc, 30-32 / Girona, 18

Roselló, 252

Hospital de Sant Pau

Diagonal, 468

Diagonal, 500

320

LA ROTONDA

Passeig de Sant Gervasi, 51-53

Provença, 185

Passeig de Gràcia, 75 / Mallorca, 275

Nàpols, 266

Rosselló, 293

París, 204

Rambla de Catalunya, 112 / Rosselló, 243-245

Bruc, 134 / Mallorca, 301

Pau Claris, 140-142

Alí Bei, 5

Còrsega, 271

Girona, 132

Girona, 120

Rosselló, 192

Rosselló, 247

Passeig de Gràcia, 94

València, 241

Rambla de Catalunya, 34

Enric Granados, 94

Rambla de Catalunya, 122

Rambla de Catalunya, 104

Llançà / Gran Via

327

INDEX OF BUILDINGS

INDEX OF ARCHITECTS

BUNKER HILL COMMUNITY COLLEGE

3 6189 00062 7231

DATE DUE

MAR 2 1 2011	

GAYLORD   PRINTED IN U.S.A.